Olde
NOTTINGHAMSHIRE
PUNISHMENTS

Ian
Morgan

Olde
NOTTINGHAMSHIRE
PUNISHMENTS

Ian Morgan

First published 2012

The History Press
The Mill, Brimscombe Port
Stroud, Gloucestershire, GL5 2QG
www.thehistorypress.co.uk

British Library Cataloguing in Publication Data.
A catalogue record for this book is available from the British Library.

ISBN 978 0 7524 5531 0

Typesetting and origination by The History Press
Printed in Great Britain

CONTENTS

ACKNOWLEDGEMENTS

I am indebted to many people for their help and understanding in assisting me in writing this book, and I have great pleasure in thanking them for their valued assistance. My special thanks go to Bingham Town Clerk, Lynn Holland, for giving me permission to photograph a cell. I would also like to thank Mark Dorrington of Nottinghamshire Archives for granting me special permission to examine and publish parts of the Southwell workhouse punishment book and, once more, I must thank Liz Weston of Mansfield Museum for the access and use of their photographic archives. The help and assistance I received from the staff of Nottingham Local Studies Library were invaluable during my visits there, as was the freedom afforded to me by Bev Baker of Nottingham Galleries of Justice, who allowed me to roam freely through the library and archives. An extra special thanks must go to Jennifer Handfield for helping me research the story of Thomas Peatfield. My thanks also go to Nick Tomlinson of Derbyshire County Council and www.picturethepast.org.uk, for allowing me to reproduce a number of photographs from within their archives. If I have missed anyone please accept my apologies – your help was invaluable.

FOREWORD

This study of the punishments of days of old should be a reminder to us that the cruelty and revengefulness of such actions were not always solutions for wrong-doers and criminals – none more so than the use of capital punishment for even the most trivial of crimes: on 27 July 1785, Thomas Cobb was executed for housebreaking:

> This malefactor was a very poor man, and had a large family. His necessities had driven him to the overseer of the parish, to which he belonged for relief; and being benighted on his return home, he called at a small public house in Normanton-upon-Trent and asked for lodgings. Being refused, he went into the yard, thinking to sleep in a stable or barn; but whilst wandering about, he saw the landlady lay her pocket in the chair under the window; and being urged by a sense of his necessities, the temptation became too strong for his resistance. The contents were of little value. This was the felony for which the poor man was sentenced to be hung. His previous good character and the extenuating circumstances of the case induced a number of gentlemen to memorialize the Judge and the Secretary of State for a commutation of the sentence; but the law was as that of Draco, written in blood. (*The Date Book of Remarkable & Memorable Events connected with Nottingham and its Neighbourhood 850-1884*, Nottingham, 1884)

Just twenty years later, on 11 March 1802, John Attenburrow was one of eleven criminals being capitally convicted. John, only fourteen years of age at the time, was sentenced to be hanged for picking the pocket of Mr John Wilcockson. Fortunately, this time round the judge showed mercy and reprieved the youthful miscreant. These two cases are a prime example of the harshness of the Bloody Code, a period between 1688 and 1815 where over 200 offences were punishable by death, regardless of the offender's age. For those who escaped such punishment, other harsh punishments were placed upon the wrong-doer; savage whippings, public humiliation and retaliation in the stocks and pillory, banishment to the unknown lands of the North Americas and Australia, and those who remained in the country had to endure dreadful prison conditions. The processes of reform and rehabilitation were yet to be associated with such institutions. Prisons were then filthy dens of iniquity, where prisoners – first-time offenders or habitual, male, female or juvenile – freely associated with one another and the use of fetters, pits, and dark cells was common practice.

However, there was a beacon of hope in the work of Britain's penal reformers. We reached a point of enlightenment by the mid-nineteenth century, brought about by the determination of penal reformers such as John Howard, Elizabeth Fry and Mary Carpenter. These philanthropists, to name a few, were an integral part in reforming our penal system, not just how we punished transgressors of the law, but also the conditions under which they were imprisoned. No longer were first-time offenders to share the cells with hardened criminals, or juveniles to suffer the conditions and sentences as adult offenders, and no longer were female prisoners to fall foul of the abuse of the male prison officers.

Therefore, whatever evil may step into the doorways of our courtrooms today, cruelty has no place in our justice and penal system, and the instruments of those punishments; the pillory, the stocks, and the gallows, should only be seen in our museums as a reminder of our forbearers' brutality.

Bev Baker,
Curator and Archivist
Galleries of Justice, Nottingham, 2012

INTRODUCTION

Crime has always been with us in one form or another and every generation has endeavoured to punish the criminal in the way that they thought most appropriate. Just about the only thing that has changed over the years is how each particular crime was perceived and how it was dealt with. During the age of the caveman, I have no doubt that these cave dwellers would from time to time, during times of shortage, steal food from their neighbours in order to survive.

In the eyes of the law today, the theft of food is treated as such a minor offence it goes almost unnoticed, while in days-gone-by, the effects could have been so catastrophic to the victim that more than likely it brought harsh and violent retribution. Yet it is, in effect, the same offence with the same loss to the victim. Many-a-time have the exasperated readers of newspapers and viewers of news seen a criminal given a seemingly lenient sentence for a serious crime only to exclaim out loud, 'Two hundred years ago, they'd have hanged them, a hundred years ago they'd have put them in prison, now it's just a warning, it'll soon be compulsory!'

Sport and recreation has always had a curious way of dividing opinion about when and where it should be played and by whom. There is no wonder then that the game of football crops up frequently in court records in such a way as to give the impression that it has always had a way of causing problems, whether it be warring players on opposing teams, over enthusiastic spectators or being the cause for dodging work. On 19 July 1621, the constable from Screveton 'was fined 4s for not presenting a riott and illegal assembly of football players in his constablewick'.

During the reign of Richard II, it was made illegal for some parts of the community (mainly servants and labourers) to play a whole range of games in order to make them take up archery, and, even though the law was repealed under James I, some labourers were still prohibited from taking part in such frivolous activities. In today's society, football is big business, and, far from being banned, it is encouraged.

Ironically, some of the most heinous of crimes used to be given the lightest of sentences by the courts. On 23 November 1541, Christopher Hogeson of East Retford attacked and assaulted Richard Westby of the same town. Using his sword, Hogeson ran Westby clean through the heart – killing him instantly. There were five witnesses to the attack, so Hogeson's guilt was never in doubt and yet at his trial, even though he was found guilty, he

Below An Entrance to Nottingham County Gaol with its corrected spelling.

Above *Nottingham House of Correction. (NTGM017628 Courtesy of Nottinghamshire County Council and www.picturethepast.org.uk)*

was only outlawed. Compare this to the tale of poor Richard Comyn who was executed at Nottingham in 1720 for 'uttering of a base shilling' (trying to pass a forged shilling coin that he was thought to have made) at Mansfield. Right up to the last, he protested over the injustice of his sentence. Of course, his numerous protestations fell on deaf ears, and the crowd enjoyed the spectacle of his hanging.

Some of the offences committed centuries ago now seem bizarre and even quaint by today's standards and the punishments handed down by each of the courts involved can also come across as somewhat strange. It must be remembered, however, that the use of capital and corporal punishment were used both as a means of inflicting retribution on the convicted, and also as a deterrent to others. Fines were, for all intents and purposes, a slap on the wrist to criminals convicted of lesser crimes with the warning not to do the same again regardless of their rank or standing in society. Temporary incarceration in a House of Correction or Gaol was for those men, women and children who had strayed from the path of goodness and had committed an offence somewhere between the two extremes. In April 1808, 'T.O.' was sent to Southwell House of Correction for six months for stealing old rope but whether this brief brush with imprisonment worked in keeping this unfortunate out of trouble is not known. Sending the guilty to gaol was believed to be a way of punishing and at the same time rehabilitating anyone who had strayed into a life of crime. Various methods and approaches of disciplining the prisoners were tried out within the walls of the prisons and gaols, as we shall see later on. Each one of these regimes that were tried out was designed to frighten or rehabilitate the criminal so that they could return into society's fold and make a useful contribution. The big question was whether any of the systems tried out ever really worked.

The varying methods of catching, prosecuting and punishing wrongdoers has changed dramatically over the passing centuries but no matter how strange the punishments meted out to law breakers appear in today's society nothing can be stranger or more outlandish than those Olde Nottinghamshire Punishments of yesteryear.

~One~

THE HISTORY BEHIND IT ALL

It is a fact of life that rules and regulations, and the threat of punishment, bring order to everyday living, even though we often wish we could disregard them. A society without laws was deemed a society cursed with the inevitable threat of anarchy; thus, systems began to evolve that tried to protect victims from aggressors.

When the Romans invaded Britain, they brought with them their own laws and methods of law enforcement to keep the population in check, which usually entailed the locals being subjected to military discipline if an uprising occurred. Any type of civil law was solely for Roman citizens who basked in a sophisticated legal system, on the other hand the local tribe of Corieltauvi (Coritani) had no recourse to the legal system of the invaders and carried on using their own tried and tested methods. Only the Romanised Britons would eventually be able to take advantage of the foreign way of law and order.

With the demise of the Roman Empire and the withdrawal of its army from Britain in AD 410, the Angles and the Saxons, both Germanic tribes, came across from the continent to fill the void bringing with them a legal system that is in part at least, still with us today.

The Anglo-Saxons divided all men over the age of twelve into groups of ten called 'tithings', from which they elected a leader, the 'tithingman'. Ten tithings collected together to form 'hundreds' which were in turn grouped into Shires and overseen by the Shire Reeve – later to become the Sheriff. Under this sophisticated system, each tithing was responsible for law and order amongst its members with any guilty party taken before the courts. In order to make everything work, sanctions were imposed against any tithing that failed to hand over one of its number if they had broken the law.

For the system to be successful, the community had to pull together to act as a unified anti-crime force, and part of its duties was to assist any victim of crime by pursuing the alleged robber when the alarm had been raised. To alert his neighbours, a victim of crime would raise a 'hue and cry' by calling out for help. Anyone within earshot was obliged at that point to drop anything they were doing and chase after the thief. If the culprit got away, the Reeve would call for everyone to join a 'posse comitatus' to pursue and catch them. With no police force to bring malefactors to justice, it was a method of law enforcement that was to have quite a surprising success rate when it was correctly put to use over the succeeding centuries.

At Balderton in 1336, a carter who saw burglars breaking into Balderton Grange was killed by the intruders; the locals who came across the ghastly scene raised a hue and cry and the chase was on. The ill-fated burglars were caught at Hawton where they were then beheaded.

By the sixteenth century, the pursuit of criminals was on a more formal footing as constables had to take up the chase along with the locals to save the Hundred from liability for any wrongdoings, and it was under Elizabeth I that it became a requirement that the hue and cry must include horsemen as well as footmen. Not all constables believed they should be under obligation to take part as the Constable of Farndon let be known in April 1609. For his lack of public spirit he was fined 3s 4d 'because when the hue and cry was sent to him by the Constable of Barneby he neglected to raise it and pursue'. On the other hand, mischief makers were also caught trying to raise a false hue and cry as in July 1615 when two labourers were prosecuted for doing just that.

For the Saxons, the highest form of judgement they had was that of judgement by God. Unresolved or difficult issues could be judged using Trial by Ordeal when an accused person underwent physical hardships to prove their innocence. In 'Trial by Cold Water', the accused was given Holy water to drink before being thrown into a river or some other large body of water. If he floated he was guilty, and, if he sank, innocent.

'Trial by Hot Water' was a very painful exercise whereby a stone was put at the bottom of a boiling cauldron of water. The accused then plunged their hand into the water to retrieve the stone, badly burning their hand in the process. The wound was then wrapped and bandaged and left alone for three days. If, on examination, after three days the hand had healed or was showing signs of recovery, the accused was given the benefit of doubt and proclaimed not guilty. If, however, the hand was infected or showed no signs of healing, it was proof of guilt.

Possibly the worst Trial by Ordeal was that of 'Trial by Iron', which required a piece of red hot iron to be carried 9ft. As in 'Trial by Hot Water', the injured hand had just three days to show improvement or guilt was presumed.

Prisons and gaols did not exist so most crimes were punishable by fines – but some did carry the death penalty. Crimes carried out against the King or crimes that could not be compensated could lead to the offender being hanged, or sometimes drowning or beheading was seen to be more appropriate. The condemned had a slim chance of being saved if their friends and relatives were able to band together to find enough money to buy their freedom.

When the Normans invaded and spread their influence throughout the countryside, they found that it was far more prudent to keep the majority of the Saxon system of law enforcement in place rather than to replace it with something that might not work. One major change that was introduced some years after the Conquest was the creation of High or Chief Constables and Petty Constables to keep order in their own locality.

High Constables first appeared after the Statute of Winchester of 1285, under Edward I, to enforce the law in the Hundreds. Whilst Petty or Parish Constables were seen as inferior to the High Constables, they had the task of arresting criminals and from the seventeenth century they had to follow the instructions of the Justices under whose control they now fell. The lack of a constable often led to social disorder, and, on 5 October 1612, the court was told by the inhabitants of Radford there were 'many nuisances and inconveniences' because of no constable being appointed. The court simply passed a judgement that one

Tuxford lock-up.

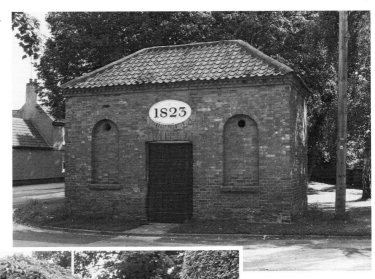

Farnsfield lock-up.

The remains of iron-securing rings in the remnants of Edwinstowe's lock-up.

must be assigned, a task that was not always easy to fulfil. Petty Constables were unpaid and took on the responsibility for a whole year, an odious task that many men did their best to get out of. John Lupton of Worksop thought he had the perfect excuse to get exemption from serving as constable when he stood in front of the court on 4 October 1633. He explained how he could not serve his term of office because he was the keeper of the deer in Sherwood Forest, and he that he should be freed from the obligation of taking the duty of constable. The court declined to accept his reasoning, and he was forced to take the job as well as fulfil the needs of his full-time occupation.

The functions that the Petty Constables had to perform ranged from keeping order and apprehending suspected felons to making sure that the accused was presented for trial. During the time that the prisoner was held before trial, it fell upon the shoulders of the constable to look after his or her welfare very often at the constable's expense, a burden that made many a constable wish that his year in office was over. Charles White of Watnall was taken to court for not paying the constable's 'wages', a situation that could have wreaked havoc if all the gentlemen of the area had followed suit, especially as the unpaid constable could often be tempted with a bribe to look the other way when circumstances required it.

With a system in place that was, at best, inefficient, and, at worst, non existent, it fell to private enterprise to employ a more professional body of law keepers. Towards the latter part of the eighteenth century, with the increased urbanisation of the population and the resultant growth in the size of the towns, momentum grew for night watchmen to take on more of the responsibility for maintaining order in towns and cities. The 'Charlies', as they became nicknamed, were financed by local businesses to protect their own town during night time when burglars and thieves roamed the streets.

Nottingham, Mansfield, and Retford all had their own night watchmen to keep guard at night and the Retford Waits, as they were called, displayed a large silver badge on their arm as proof of their office and to show their authority in apprehending suspected malefactors.

A meeting held in Nottingham in 1788 decided that an arrangement of volunteers should police property, a system that was doomed to failure, so they tried again. This time, they employed the watchmen to look after the properties of the businessmen who paid their wages, another system with failings as the watchmen would decline to act if they saw burglars at work on the property of a non-subscriber to the scheme. In the end, the Watching and Warding Act of 1816 was passed whereby any inhabitant over the age of seventeen and party to the poor rate had to take part in protecting the town at night. Groups of twenty-five citizens would patrol the area to protect property, but such a large body of people invariably had the effect of warning any burglars that they were in the area as they made their way around non-too-quietly. Refusal to join in the guarding of the town had the potential to lead to a fine ranging anywhere from £2 all the way up to £10. In the end, Nottingham's watchmen would gain the enviable reputation of being an efficient body.

One of the difficulties facing both the constables and the night watchmen after detaining a criminal was what they should do with them. Gaols and prisons were generally used to house those awaiting trial and for the long term incarceration of debtors, but the big problem facing the lawmen was how to get the prisoners there. Some of those that

Above *Bingham's Old Court House.*

Right *The cell door in Bingham Court House.*

were arrested were no more than drunkards that just needed to be locked up over night to sober up and so anyone captured invariably spent at least one night in the village lock-up, a secure building designed to hold prisoners until they could be delivered to court to face trial. Naturally enough, the drunkards were let out the following day to go back to work – hangover and all. Most towns and villages had their own lock-ups many of which have now gone, the only ones still standing in Nottinghamshire are at Tuxford, Farnsfield, Mansfield Woodhouse, and the remains of one at Edwinstowe. Tuxford's village lock-up was rather forward thinking for its day with two cells, each having its own privy. As crude and basic as most of them were, these small lock-ups did what was required of them for many years until the inception of a professional police force with secure facilities.

Those charged with offences were taken before one of three different types of court, each one dealing with crimes of a successively more serious nature. The lowest level of court was the Petty Sessions where minor offences were tried or where cases were to be judged to see whether a higher court should hear the trial. The Quarter Sessions followed, which, as the name suggests, took place at regular intervals four times a year. Crimes that were of a more serious nature were held there amidst the prospect of more harsh punishments. The highest of the three courts was the Assizes where the most serious and horrific crimes, from murder to robbery, were tried and with the severity and importance of the trials uppermost the location of the courts was limited to Retford, Newark and more frequently at Nottingham.

The towns of Nottinghamshire became equipped with their own courthouses to deal with the minor crimes – each one having cells inside the same building or nearby. Bingham, Mansfield, Retford, Southwell, Newark and Nottingham all had their own courthouses and the conditions in which the supposed offenders were kept was meant to be adequate rather than comfortable.

With courthouses and gaols improving with their dealing with felons and their punishments, it became increasingly obvious that the days of the Petty Constables and watchmen were numbered. The age of the hue and cry had been overtaken by an increase in population and the movement of labour away from the countryside and into the towns and cities. What was needed was a new way of policing an ever-increasing and unruly populace that needed to be kept in check.

Part of the Municipal Corporations Act of 1835 required boroughs to set up a system of efficient policing; however, it was not until the Rural Constabulary Act of 1839, which allowed Justices of the Peace in England and Wales to set up rural police forces, that any real progress was made. This was not a compulsory measure and relied on the will of the Justices to follow it through, but the final piece of legislation that brought about a formal police force in Nottinghamshire was the 1856 County and Borough Police Act, which required every county to set up its own police force if it had not already done so.

In 1836, Newark, Retford and Nottingham had each set up borough police forces to combat the escalating crime wave rippling throughout the early Victorian Britain, and they were soon followed in 1840 by the

Nottinghamshire Constabulary. This embryonic force began with just forty-two officers (a Chief Constable, eight Superintendents and thirty-three constables) for the whole county but within the year they had been joined by the Retford Borough Police, thereby increasing their numbers. It was becoming increasingly obvious that the policeman on the beat did not have the time or facilities to investigate many of the large crimes he attended, so, in 1854, Nottingham Borough Police set up the first criminal investigation department in the county.

The early days of the Nottingham Police had not run entirely smoothly as a number of incidents came to light. In 1838, Inspector Wilson was taken to task and reprimanded for being a little too enthusiastic over an investigation into a robbery whilst four constables were more than happy to receive £19 as a reward for capturing a known criminal – unfortunately, a watch house keeper by the name of George Spybey was dismissed for not doing his job properly and letting the man abscond.

For many years, Nottinghamshire was a mixture of separate forces until the Newark Borough Police joined the Nottinghamshire Constabulary in 1947, and, finally, in 1968, the Nottinghamshire Constabulary merged with the Nottingham City Police to make the police force that we know today.

Two

CORPORAL PUNISHMENT

The old saying, 'If you can't beat them, join them' was not the sort that the courts and law enforcers wanted to see displayed amongst the criminal fraternity as they tried desperately to keep order in the towns and countryside. A more accurate axiom that they lived by would have been 'to stop them being joined, beat them', as they dished out large amounts of corporal punishment to all and sundry. The rough-and-ready justice of corporal punishment was designed to hurt and publicly humiliate those on the receiving end as well as acting as a deterrent for onlookers. In most cases, the spectacle of seeing someone in receipt of a good bashing, whacking or soaking more often than not offered the spectators with a good day out, and seldom prevented them from committing a crime.

The Cuck-Stool

In its early days the cuck-stool, or cucking stool, was used for distinctly different reasons to the ducking stool and only with the slow passage of time did these two types of punishment merge into one. Both sorts of stool followed a similar design whereby the unlucky perpetrator was tied in a chair like seat at the end of a long pole, very much like a see-saw. Unlike the ducking stool that was used to plunge the guilty in and out of decidedly cold water, the cuck-stool was used as a means of humiliating the culprit in front of their own doors or some other public place. The hopefully degrading spectacle of the ducking stool was mainly used for the silencing of scolds, who often tittle-tattled to the annoyance of their neighbours, but other crimes could also be punished in this way. Under a law passed by Henry VIII, any carders or spinners who had been found guilty of fraud were to be 'sett [sic] upon the pillory or cukkyng-stole, [sic] man or woman, as the case shall require'.

In January 1619, Anna Sugar of Arnold incensed the locals to such an extent that she was taken to court and sentenced to 'be dipped tomorrow in ye cuckstool [sic] for scolding', and all would have been well for Grace Heefield of Worksop if she had kept her thoughts to herself – instead, her wagging tongue led her to 'suffer penalty in the cuckstoole [sic]'.

Once in a while, long-suffering, hen-pecked husbands plucked up the courage to complain about their treatment at home, and, in October 1612, one unnamed labourer found he had had enough and won his case against his nagging wife and had her cucked 'for being a common scold in her house'. It is not recorded whether his wife learned her

A seventeenth-century woodcut of the cucking stool.

lesson, or if he was too frightened to attempt a trip to court for a second time.

Judges sometimes passed the sentence of cucking only to find that the implement of punishment did not exist in that particular place, much to the dismay of the town or village involved. Fiskerton fell foul of the expense of providing a cucking stool in 1680 after the successful prosecution of Elizabeth Leeming, when the judge ordered the locals to, 'erect a cuckstoole [*sic*] within a fortnight upon ye penalty of £5 and that ye wife Elizabeth Leeming be cucked three times by ye constable of said towne [*sic*]'.

The cucking stool was quite plainly a popular form of punishment, as the many letters of complaint about the lack of a local stool from various inhabitants clearly show. One court entry tells of a complaint filed by the constable and inhabitants of Southwell in October 1654, who bemoaned their inability to chastise scolds and brawling women who disturbed the peace because their cuck-stool had been destroyed during the Civil War. Since its loss, they claimed lewd and 'turbulent' women had become more brazen and open while performing their trade, much to the distress of law-abiding citizens of the town. The court agreed with the plaintiffs and gave an order that a new stool must be made and placed in the same location that the old one had stood. Unfortunately for Elizabeth Banes, almost a year to the day later, she was found guilty of brawling and such noisy activities that her neighbours found that going about their normal daily lives in peace very difficult. Banes ended up at the wrong end of the new cucking stool as the onlookers no doubt gleefully watched.

Mayor Thomas Trigge

Situated in an area called Cook Stool Row, Nottingham's cuck-stool was a strange contraption that could accommodate two unwilling participants in a seat that resembled a hollow box with holes in the side, through which the culprits put their heads. This large object of punishment bore more resemblance to a mobile pillory than a method of soaking a wrongdoer in cold water. In 1731, Mayor Thomas Trigge concluded that a woman of low moral standing must pay for her failings by being publicly 'cucked' in the Row. Although unused for some time, the cuck-stool was produced and the woman was handed over to the mob, who fixed her in the seat and mercilessly began to duck her in and out of the water. The poor woman was ducked so severely that she died a short time later, causing Mayor Trigge a great deal of trouble. Trigge was prosecuted for being the instigator of her death, and the authorities ordered the cuck-stool to be destroyed and the pond filled in. Cook Stool Row was later renamed The Poultry, but the memory of the area's former past is still remembered in Poynton Street, which was named after a widow Poynton who was on the wrong end of the cuck-stool after she was ducked in 1609 for being a scold.

The Pillory

As a tool of public humiliation and punishment, the pillory was an ideal weapon in the armoury of justice, as it fulfilled two basic requirements – it was cheap to use and the assembled crowd that had turned out to watch were the ones that actually meted out the punishment. Traditionally designed to accommodate one or two felons, the pillory consisted of an upright pole on top of which were two pieces of wood joined at one end by a hinge. Fashioned into the wood were a number of holes – one for the head and one for each wrist – through which the criminal placed their limbs. When the upper piece of wood was lowered and locked into position, the reluctant sufferer would stand and wait for whatever was to come.

The entertainment value for the crowd came when they were allowed to throw anything that came to hand at the offenders; the usual missiles were rotten fruit, vegetables and eggs, but it was not at all uncommon for dead animals, mud, offal and human excrement to be thrown. If the criminal had been involved in a particularly unsavoury crime, or they had enemies in the crowd, then bricks, rocks and stones were the order of the day, which could, and very often did, lead to death. Conversely, if the convicted criminal was well liked, or their crime was deemed as petty, then they could expect to be left alone or pelted with flowers or posies. Whatever the crime, or whoever the criminal was, one thing was guaranteed and that was a good turn out because the pillory was always sited in a very public area. It is clear to see how popular this type of punishment was purely because of the length of time the pillory was in use. Retford received permission to use the cuck-stool and pillory in November 1279, during the reign of Edward I, and it was still in use many years later.

Many crimes were punishable by an hour in the pillory such as fraud, perjury, speaking badly of the Crown, sedition or felony. On more rare occasions, the term of punishment would be increased to reflect the severity of the crime.

William Boardman had an early release from gaol in October 1632, after being convicted of perjury, when it was found too expensive to keep him locked up in

A pillory.

A combined stocks, pillory and whipping post.

prison, so he was brought to Mansfield on market day and put in the pillory for one hour instead.

The pillory became useful in 1690 when Daniel Clay spoke too loudly and openly against King William and Queen Mary, his sentence to be set in the pillory from midday to 1 p.m. on the next market day with this inscription placed on his forehead: 'For speaking these words, God damn King William and Queen Mary and King James should and would come again'.

Perjury seems to have been a common offence, for, in 1633, Gabriel Eaton of Trowell had to stand in Bingham's pillory in the market but wily John Stephenson must have thought he had come up with a foolproof way of avoiding being pelted while undertaking his time fastened in the pillory. On 16 October 1776, as he mounted the steps leading to his humiliation, he turned to the watching crowd and raising his clenched fists aloft he clearly let it be known that if anyone dare throw anything at him he would seek them out and make them pay. For almost three quarters of an hour, the subdued crowd remained quiet until at last the peace was broken and a bombardment of unmentionables went Stephenson's way.

John Kitchen's Ears

The use of the pillory was restricted to the castigation of perjurers after 1816. In 1837, it was finally abolished, but, during its heyday, judges sometimes added a twist to the sentence. At the trial of John Kitchen from Mansfield, on 9 July 1638, he was found guilty of perjury, whereupon the judge ordered he be sent to gaol without any chance of bail. After nine days, Kitchen was taken by the Sheriff to the pillory in the market place where he was to stand 'for the space of two hours together, having both ears fastened to the same pillory with nails according to the statute'.

The Unfortunate James Knight

Instead of living a nice quiet life, James Knight of Wollaton thought it would be a good idea to indulge in a little blackmail. However, choosing William Bingham as his target, it soon became clear that he had chosen the wrong man. Knight falsely accused Bingham of buggery with a cow and in order to keep quiet about it he demanded money in return. Sadly for Knight, Bingham reported him and soon the blackmailer was in the dock where he was quickly found guilty. At noon on 24 July 1773, Knight was placed in the pillory where he stood for a full thirty minutes with a huge crowd watching and waiting expectantly as nothing happened. After the half hour had passed, Knight, who must have thought he had escaped unscathed, was put on the receiving end of a barrage of 'rotten eggs, dirt and sludge' that lasted for the remaining half hour of his sentence. He was later taken back to the county gaol to start a twelve-month sentence – possibly more humbled, but definitely smellier.

The Finger Pillory (Finger Stocks)

Victorian school children were often kept in check by the use of the finger pillory. Mainly used in upper class schools, but also used in churches and on servants, the finger pillory trapped the fingers inside a hinged wooden block, bent at the middle joint. The disorderly child had to endure this painful punishment until remorse was shown, or their class work improved. Adults and children failing to take note of the sermon in church, and inattentive servants, frequently found themselves facing a spell with their fingers imprisoned.

The Stocks

One of the oldest forms of corporal punishment in use throughout the country were the stocks – indeed, there is evidence that the Anglo-Saxons used them on many occasions. Unlike the pillory that pinioned the wrongdoer by the neck and wrists, the stocks held the captive in place by holding his or her legs secure whilst they remained in a seated position. Not only were the stocks used as a means of punishment where the culprit was publicly ridiculed and pelted with all manner of unmentionables, but they were also used as a way of securely holding prisoners before they went to trial. In 1351, during the reign of Edward III, the Second Statute of Labourers Act allowed any troublesome labourer to be stocked, and in 1405 it was made law that every town and village must provide a set or face punishment. The good people of Everton were fined in 1653 for not having a pair of stocks, while the inhabitants of South Scarle were prosecuted for not providing enough stocks. Many crimes were punishable by spending a few hours in the stocks ranging from theft and vagrancy all the way up to blasphemy. James I declared in 1605 that anyone convicted of being a drunkard should be fined 5s or spend six hours in the stocks.

Whipping was commonly given as part of the punishment to anyone placed in the stocks, as Robert Key and Elizabeth Lamyng from Ratcliffe were to discover in April 1613, when they were sentenced to three hours in the stocks during the 'time of service' and to be stripped to the waist and whipped.

Sometimes the judge who passed sentence had a curious sense of humour and justice as shown in the case of Suzan Tomy from Laneham who had to endure three hours in the stocks for stealing a child's blanket with the damning evidence placed in front of her as a constant reminder.

A harsh reminder of the difficulties of being without work was brought home to Edward Beecham, his wife Ellen, Anne Hodgson, and Margaret Knowles when they discovered they were all to be placed in the stocks at Bleasby for vagrancy in April 1655. Despite each of the women having a child, all four of the culprits were publicly stripped to the waist and whipped. Upon their release, they were each sent back to the place of their origin.

Nottingham's last use of the stocks came on 6 April 1808, when a Scotsman by the name of Calvin was taken by cart from the gaol to Nottingham market place. Found guilty of offences against children, he arrogantly bowed to the crowd before taking his place in full view of the huge assembled mass. When his hour was up, he remounted the cart and was taken back to gaol to finish off his sentence. By now, the use of the pillory was so rare it had been nearly sixty years since Nottingham had last used it.

Cart Tails and Whipping Posts

Henry VIII's Whipping Act of 1530 laid down very strict rules that all vagrants, regardless of sex, should be stripped naked, tied to the tail of a cart and whipped constantly as they were paraded through the town. The whipping was only to end when 'the body shall be bloody by reason of such whipping' and, afterwards, the unfortunate sufferer had to take an oath to acknowledge that they would return to the place of their birth or to the place that they had last lived at for a total of three years. It was during the reign of Elizabeth I that the Act was amended, so that those to be whipped were only naked from the waist upwards and the use of the cart was abolished to be replaced by a whipping post.

The use of the whip was a well-established method of retribution even before the 1530 Act, as Cecily of Staunton found out to her cost. During July 1299, Cecily was shown to be guilty of having an adulterous affair with William de Breadon. The Archbishop of York ordered Cecily to be whipped for a duration of six days at the church at Staunton, and, to top it off, she had to undergo the same beatings in Nottingham and Bingham market places. De Breadon must have had quite a feisty temper, because he made the messenger delivering the summons eat it. For his troubles, De Breadon was excommunicated.

The crimes punishable by a whipping were wide and varied, and, by later standards, unjustified in their severity, when such crimes as being a vagrant, being the parents of a bastard and selling ale without a licence brought the full force of the law down on the malefactor.

In July 1693, Ffrances Holmes of Elton, who mothered a bastard child, was ordered to be tied to a cart tail, stripped to the waist and to be soundly whipped from one end of the town to the other.

A prisoner receiving a whipping.

Scolds Bridle

A brank, or scold's bridle.

The Nottingham Brank, 1895.

Trying to escape justice has always brought down stiffer penalties on any criminal, but Anthony Yates must have concluded he had managed to evade justice when he escaped from gaol. On 11 April 1774, Yates was committed to the County Gaol on a charge of vagrancy, yet the wily Yates had no intention of completing his sentence and escaped. After a spell of freedom, he was recaptured and, in July of the following year, he found himself in court once again. On this occasion, he was given six months in the House of Correction and ordered to be whipped at Bingham, Southwell and Newark on market days.

Whipping was also commonplace during the nineteenth century, especially for the younger members of society. In March 1839, William Tomkins (14) was sent to prison for one week and soundly whipped once for stealing a coat, while James Banner (14) was also locked up for a week and soundly whipped once for sealing two musical boxes.

A Drink to the Pretender

Military justice can be harsh and swift, as shown in one particular incident that took place in Nottingham. During their time in Nottingham in July 1737, Lord Cadogan's Regiment were witness to a dragoon from their ranks receiving 300 lashes for drinking to the health of the Pretender. His punishment continued in Derby, where he received another 300 lashes, after which he had a halter placed around his neck and was drummed out of the Regiment.

The Brank

Known more commonly as the Scold's Bridle, the brank was a device used on women accused of gossip and spreading rumours, and sometimes on women who upset their husbands by continually talking or complaining. Comprising of a metal frame that fitted around the head and fastened in place by means of a lock, it had at its front a large plate, which was either sharpened or had a spike on it that went inside the woman's mouth. Any movement of the tongue caused severe pain as the spike dug into the tender flesh, so it was better to keep quiet, generally to the relief of the neighbourhood.

Without doubt, the most renowned person to be subject to the Nottingham brank was not a woman but a man. James Brodie, a blind beggar, had stood trial for the murder of his young guide boy, William Henesal, in July 1799; it was claimed he had beaten the eight-year-old to death. The jury rejected his defence that the boy had fallen from a tree, and found him guilty as charged. Condemned to be hanged, he was taken back to the gaol to await his date with the hangman where he began such a tirade of language and created so much of a nuisance that he was placed in the brank. Brodie was hanged on 15 July, a mere three days after his trial.

It was during a visit to Nottingham in 1821, that Judge Richardson ordered the brank to be destroyed, but, unusually, it appears that Nottingham might have had a second brank in use because years later another Judge at the Assizes, Baron Parke, came across the implement whilst on a visit to the gaol. Appalled that the brank was still available for use, he gave the order to 'Take away that relic of barbarism'. Not willing to destroy it, one of the guardians of the gaol, John Sanders, took it home.

Birching

Generally reserved for wayward children, the birching rod consisted of a bunch of twigs tied together to make an implement that was used against the bare buttocks of the offender. Used to keep minors in check, it was meant to be a short sharp shock that would put them back on the straight and narrow; something that did not always work.

Frederick Scraton of Southwell was given six strokes of the birch in 1898 when aged twelve, and a further twelve strokes in 1899. Samuel Trout of Nottingham was an even younger offender who had received six strokes on three separate occasions before 1899 when he was only eleven years old.

The 'Monocled Mutineer'

As a boy, Percy Toplis was already quite a character. In 1908, he appeared before the Mansfield Petty Sessions. Aged just eleven, he was charged with obtaining goods by false pretences after convincing a tailor that he had been sent to pick up two sets of boys' clothing. Making a smooth getaway, he put on one of the suits and pawned

Percy Toplis, the 'Monacled Mutineer'.

Branding in court.

the other. It was not long before Toplis was caught and tried, with his punishment being six strokes of the birch. Sadly this was to be the start – and not the end – of a short but turbulent life that ended when Toplis was killed in a police shootout in 1920 following his escapades during the First World War, when he took part in an army mutiny.

Branding

Given as a deliberately painful penalty for law-breaking, branding also advertised to the world that the person before them was a convicted felon. Under the Statute of Vagabonds, introduced by Edward VI, anyone out of work for three days could be sold into slavery for two years after first having a letter 'V' burned into their shoulder. If the slave managed to escape, they had to undergo further pain while a letter 'S' was burned into their forehead or cheek, to show to the world at large their status in life. 'Incorrigible vagabonds' had the letter 'R' burned into the shoulders or arms, while a thief received a 'T'. Sentences were carried out in the court but it has been suggested that those convicted, who had ready money, would bribe the executioner to use a cool branding iron. The branding of prostitutes had to be halted after it was discovered they had been using the branding mark as a sign of their profession and used it as an advertisement.

An 'incorrigible vagabond' was brought before the courts at Nottingham, in July 1615, and was sentenced to be 'then and there in court with a hot burning hent [sic] a large Roman letter R be impressed the size of a shilling on his left arm' after which the culprit was sent back to his or her place of origin. Just two years later, another wrongdoer was branded in the same courthouse as a vagabond on the left shoulder.

On 18 April 1634, Joell Sleeford narrowly escaped the death penalty after he had been found guilty of the capital crime of stealing three sheep. Pleading Benefit of Clergy he successfully read out the 'neck verse', but, as a parting shot, the judge ordered him to be branded on the right hand.

Branding was such a common punishment that, in Nottingham, it was securely fixed to the front of the dock in readiness to be used and it was not a cheap implement to use. In February 1772, Anne Taylor was branded on the hand for some unknown crime and the cost to the court amounted to 5s. Her subsequent imprisonment turned out to be far more expensive because seven months later, while still incarcerated, Taylor gave birth to a child. Her medical costs totalled £3 9s.

Gradually, the use of the branding iron faded out until it was abolished in 1829.

—Three—

CAPITAL PUNISHMENT

Say it Again

The implementation of the death sentence led to an assortment of proverbs and superstitions that have entered into the English language, and are still in everyday use from one end of the country to the other. The question is, do you know which ones they are? There is no true definition as to the origin to many of these proverbs and sayings, but those most associated with capital punishment offer the most entertaining reasons – whether they are correct or not. Here a few of the more popular ones:

To be *on the wagon* comes from the time when prisoners on their way to the place of execution were placed in the back of a cart or wagon. Traditionally, those condemned to be hanged were allowed one last drink at an ale house on the route to the scene of their demise. After taking their last drink, they would climb back onto the cart and be *back on the wagon,* with no chance of another drink. In Nottingham, the last public house before reaching Gallows Hill was the Nags Head on Mansfield Road. There is a story of how one poor unfortunate was so eager to get the whole thing over and done with he could not face his last drink, and so by-passed this last watering hole. Moments after he was sent into oblivion at the end of the rope, a rider galloped up waving his reprieve. Perhaps he should have had that last drink after all.

As we all well know, walking under a ladder can bring untold bad luck, unless you are careful, but it appears this innocent action could stem from the time when those to be hanged had to walk up a ladder with the rope already around their neck — the other end previously thrown over a suitably sturdy branch or beam above. When the prisoner and the hangman had reached a suitable height (on the same ladder), the rope would be adjusted. The executioner then made his way to the uppermost part of the gallows, held the prisoner's shoulders steady as the hangman's assistant twisted the ladder from beneath the condemned person's feet and he was *turned off.* At this point, it was definitely bad luck for the prisoner to be underneath the ladder.

Once the prisoner had been sent towards his or her doom, death was usually an unmercifully long time in coming. It could take up to fifteen minutes for the felon to expire, and some of the worst cases saw it take up to thirty minutes, and for most of that time the prisoner would writhe and wriggle as they died of slow strangulation. If they were fortunate enough to have some money, they would pay a willing entrepreneur to pull down hard on their flailing legs to hasten their end. These people became known as *hangers on* – a term now used for someone who stays close when it suits them but is actually doing you no good. Occasionally, some good or kind relative would perform the odious task for no recompense. In 1732, William Pycroft became the last person in Nottingham to be *turned off* when he was executed at Gallows Hill for coining. It is not known if he had any *hangers on*.

To *pull the other one* sounds like a humorous jest nowadays, but many years ago it had another meaning. Originally, *to pull the other one,* was to make someone look foolish and it was thought that if a *hanger on* pulled on one leg he could induce another person to pull on the other leg by claiming he had heard money jangling in the soon-to-be-dead person's pockets, and if it fell out it was theirs.

The origin of *third time lucky* might have been forgotten but it may well have come about because of the belief that, under English law, anyone successfully surviving execution three times would automatically have their sentence commuted to life imprisonment.

Hanging

For many years, hanging was seen as the main form of punishment for crimes committed – a deterrent in the fight against crime, with no other suitable method of penalty deemed sufficiently harsh enough. At one time, it seemed that anyone with power had the right to set up a gallows and to execute the guilty. Not only did the King have the privilege to set up gallows, but so did the Church and some local dignitaries.

The Church used their right to carry out hangings if the condemned had been caught on their lands. In the thirteenth century, the Priory at Blythe was one of those orders that

An execution.

used its right to execute thieves and robbers that were caught in the liberty of Blythe, when they would take the prisoner to Emmeslowe (Blythe Law Hill) and use the gallows erected there. On one occasion, the bailiffs captured a cutpurse that had been plying his trade in the market, only to have him taken away by the steward of nearby Tickhill and to the castle there. The prior turned down an offer of 5s for the cutpurse and had him executed straight away.

There have been many sites for gallows in Nottinghamshire, but by far the most used have been that on Gallows Hill in Nottingham, the Shire Hall, the House of Correction and Bagthorpe Gaol – each one used in its day as the principal place of execution. The earliest recorded official execution in Nottinghamshire is of John de Cuckney, who was executed in Nottingham in 1201, for stealing from Ralph de Edwinstowe.

After 1660, the number of offences carrying the death penalty rose steadily until 1815, by which stage there were over 280. The 'Bloody Code', as it became known, was designed to incite fear and act as a deterrent. Some of the more unusual capital offences included; impersonating a Chelsea pensioner, going about in disguise (having a dirty or blackened face), putting graffiti on Westminster Bridge, breaking a sapling tree and the list goes on. There were so many capital crimes it was theoretically possible to be tried and executed twice for one offence. In fairness, the death penalty was rarely used in the more obscure crimes, and hanging was kept mainly for the major crimes such as murder, arson, theft and so on. It was not unknown for burglars and thieves to escape the gallows when the jury purposely valued the stolen goods at less than 2s 6d (the traditional value of goods above which the death sentence was mandatory). Occasionally, the jurors would have a whip round and compensate the robbery victim to the value of the goods lost so that the charges would be dropped.

The Short Drop

The short drop was exactly as it implies – the rope used to execute the convicted was of minimal length with little slack, and those unfortunate enough to die this way could linger for an inordinate length of time. The short drop was administered by either turning the prisoner off of a ladder (as described above), or by moving away the cart they had been transported in from beneath the gallows while they stood at the rear with the rope around their neck. Sometimes the executioner was not particularly skilled in their profession, and mishaps often occurred.

On 27 March 1782, Cooper Hall was taken to the traditional execution site at Gallows Hill, when, in an attempt to cheat fate, he grabbed the rope as the cart moved from beneath his feet. This caused the knot to slip round to the back of his neck and made for an excruciatingly slow death.

Some of those who had a date with the executioner went to their deaths with an air of bravado and an apparent lack of concern. Thomas Henfrey and William Rider were found guilty of highway robbery, and, on 23 March 1785, as they made their way to the gallows, riding on the back of the cart while attired in their shrouds, they both appeared more concerned about the friends they were leaving behind than their own fate. As the cart stood beneath the gallows and with Henfrey and Rider waiting with the ropes around their necks, Henfrey turned to Rider and smiling he asked if he would make 'a spring of it'. Rider agreed whereupon Henfrey leaped out of the cart shouting, 'then come along'.

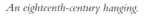

An eighteenth-century hanging.

County Hall, c.1750.

There was an audible crack and Henfrey was dead almost immediately, the rope stretching so much his feet nearly touched the ground. Rider's nerve gave out and he waited until the cart was moved away, ensuring he suffered a slow agonising death.

The Long Drop

Not everyone was satisfied that the short drop was a humane method of implementing the death sentence, and, by 1872, a new way of dispatching criminals had come to the fore. William Marwood, a boot and shoe maker from Horncastle, Lincolnshire, had devised a new method of execution using a rope long enough to allow the prisoner to fall between 6 and 10ft, taking into account his or her height and weight, which appeared to kill instantly. Initially it was thought that it brought about instant death by breaking the neck, subsequent evidence has shown that death is still caused by asphyxiation, but the condemned is unconscious during the process. Marwood, who had no previous experience as an executioner, was allowed to try out his new *long drop* method at Lincoln prison on 1 April 1872 on the murderer William Frederick Harry. The enthusiastic amateur's theories were correct, and the execution was deemed a great success by all those who witnessed it.

After being convicted of killing Ann Mellors of Car Colston, Thomas Gray became Marwoods first Nottinghamshire 'client' when he was hanged at the County Gaol in Nottingham on 21 November 1877. This was to be Nottinghamshire's first hanging to be performed away from public view and large tarpaulins were used to shield the execution yard from prying eyes. Following tradition, Gray's coffin was filled with quicklime before in was interred within the confines of the gaol.

Marwood's last visit to Nottingham was just four years later when he officiated at the hanging of Thomas Brown who had slashed the throat of his mistress, Elizabeth Caldwell, after a drunken argument.

Left *William Marwood.*

Below *The Shire Hall, Nottingham.*

The abolition of hanging in England was finally ratified by Parliament in 1969, after an experimental five-year period under the terms of the Murder (Abolition of Death Penalty) Act of 1965.

The very last execution to take place in Nottingham was carried out on 10 April 1928, when George Frederick Walter Hayward faced the hangman at Bagthorpe gaol for the murder of Mrs Amy Collinson.

The Unfortunate John Miller

John Miller, who was accused of stealing three cows from Mr Vessey of Rufford, was taken to his place of execution on 16 August 1797. He had the (mis)fortune for the rope to break after about two minutes. Placed back in the cart, he was soon brought back to his senses and was able to talk. It was not unknown at this point for the crowd, and sometimes the officials, to take pity on the convict and to spare their lives in the belief they had suffered enough already. Unfortunately for Miller, a rope-maker called Godber was in the crowd and he volunteered his services to repair the rope. Miller was then hanged for a second time – on this occasion, it was successful. Benjamin Renshaw of Mansfield might also have suffered less if fate had not lent him a hand. At his execution in 1812, the noose on the rope slipped up and over his chin as he was being turned off the cart. He was quickly pulled back into the cart and turned off for a second time.

A Killer with a Conscience

As Robert Bamford sat in his cell waiting to start his seven-year sentence of transportation for felony, his demeanour become more and more despondent. After three days of dejected deliberation, he called for the turnkey. Telling his gaoler that he had to unburden his mind, he was quizzed about the nature of his problem. A confession? Yes, and what a confession. He told how over three years earlier on 18 September 1818, he and two others, Adam Adie and William Knight, had gone out drinking with John Timms. In Jones' eating house on Parliament Row, Timms paid for all the purchases but at their next watering hole, The Three Horse Shoes at Trent Bridge, he refused to, saying he had already paid out enough. Even when pressed to by the others he stood by his decision. When the group left the inn and made their way across the bridge Adie, Knight and Bamford turned on Timms, beat him, and threw him over the parapet into the water. Drinkers in the ale houses at each end of the bridge heard the cry of 'murder' but found no evidence of any wrong-doing. The next day, two of the attackers were arrested and interviewed but with no proof against them of any crime they were released.

A few days later on the 28th September, a huge explosion on a nearby wharf at Holmepierrepont shook the air and that is when Timms' body was found floating in the Trent. The inquest jury could not decide how he had died, and so Bamford and Adie were re-examined. With no evidence against them, the men were once again set free.

It was not until Bamford's attack of remorse surfaced that the truth finally came out. Bamford, Knight and Adie were all put on trial, and, while Knight was acquitted for lack of evidence, the other two culprits were adjudged guilty and hanged on 22 March 1822. All three men would never have stood trial for Timms death if it had not been for a killer with a conscience.

Don't Upset the In-Laws

Not everyone gets on with their in-laws, but for William Healey it was to prove a fatal mistake. Standing trial in March 1793 for stealing a cow belonging to Mr Baron Thompson from Yorkshire, it looked like the evidence was flimsy and weak; Healey's father-in-law then stepped up to give evidence on behalf of the prosecution. Without the intervention of his wife's father, Healey's life would have been spared – alas, with the damning words echoing around the courtroom, Healey's unfortunate fate was sealed. There must have been some sympathy for him among the locals; on the day of the execution, a large crowd turned out to watch. It took nearly two hours for the procession to travel from the gaol to Gallows Hill.

He Did Not Want to Die

William Hill had no intention of keeping his date with the hangman, and, naturally, he did everything within his power to put off all that was due to befall him. After being convicted of the rape of Sarah Justice, he was sentenced to be hanged – when the date finally arrived in August 1803, however, he refused to leave his cell. Six wardens had to drag him from his cell and keep him under control, and, to make sure he did not jump from the cart that was to transport him to the gallows, he was chained to it. Once at the execution site, he made a desperate bid for freedom and in the ensuing chaotic fracas that followed, he had to be liberally clubbed until he was at last subdued.

Peine Forte et Dure

Peine forte et dure (strong and hard punishment) is more commonly known as 'pressing to death'. This was both a torture and a punishment which was given to those accused of a felony and who refused to plead either guilty or not guilty. It was also given to anyone who challenged more than twenty prospective jurors in the belief that the objector was time-wasting in an effort to hold up court proceedings. First introduced in 1275, by the Statute of Westminster, *Peine* was simple imprisonment and starvation until the accused gave in and submitted a plea. A change of the law in 1406 introduced the use of heavyweights as an extra element of hardship.

The refusal of the accused to enter a plea generally stemmed from that person trying to save his or her family's lands and monies from forfeiture to the state. Anyone found

Pressing to death.

guilty of a crime would lose the entire family's wealth, on top of any punishment imposed as a penalty in relation to the alleged crime itself. The absence of a plea, and subsequent death by pressing, meant that no trial had actually taken place and the accused person's family could retain their wealth. The stark and terrible words of the judge as he passed his sentence of *Peine forte et dure* would have shaken the hardiest of souls:

> That the prisoner shall be remanded to the place from whence he came, and put in some low, dark room; that he shall lie without any litter or anything under him, and that one arm shall be drawn to one quarter of the room with a cord, and the other to another, and that his feet shall be used in the same manner, and that as many weights shall be laid on him as he can bear, and more. That he shall have three morsels of barley bread a day, and that he shall have the water next the prison, so that it be not current, and that he shall not eat on the same day on which he drinks, nor drink on the same day he eats; and he shall continue until he die or answer.

At the Nottingham Assizes of 1735, an unnamed man stood in the dock accused of murder. Despite pleas from his lawyer to the judge that the defendant was unable to speak, he was sentenced to *Peine forte et dure* in an endeavour to make him enter a plea. Throughout his ordeal the accused man never spoke and, eventually, the weights he bore on his chest were too great and he was crushed to death. It later came to light that the two witnesses who claimed to have heard him speak may have been lying, and that he really had been deaf and dumb. Pressing to death was abolished in 1772 when it was decided that to remain silent was an admission of guilt.

The Rebel Stone
South of Tuxford at the side of the old Great North Road stands a large marker stone on which was originally placed the simple inscription: 'Here lieth the body of a rebel – 1745'. As a group of Jacobite prisoners were being transported to the Tower of London, with the ominous threat of possible execution, one or more of them decided to try and escape. One of the rebels fell from the cart while trying to flee and fell to the ground, breaking his neck. A local man was paid a shilling to dig a grave, and, when it was large enough, the Scotsman was interred in an upright position and given a simple form of military funeral at the place where he met his death. Tuxford's town drum was also brought out to add to the occasion. No-one knows who the dead man was, but it is generally believed he was either of noble birth or a high ranking officer. Anyone of lesser standing would not have had such an elaborate send off, nor such a fancy red stone marker, which is made from stone not found in the area.

Scottish drovers who passed the stone would chip away at it either to deface something they thought to be an insult or, more likely, to use the chippings as a safeguard against toothache.

Hanging, Drawing and Quartering
This was the ultimate in punishments, specifically reserved for men who had committed high treason. Its especially barbaric and painful process of torture, leading to eventual death, was designed to act as a deterrent to anyone proposing or taking part in treasonable

The Rebel Stone.

acts against the state, or directly against the monarch. The words that the guilty heard as sentence was passed must surely have struck fear into all except the very brave or the very foolhardy:

> That you be drawn on a hurdle to the place of execution where you shall be hanged by the neck and being alive cut down, your privy members shall be cut off and your bowels taken out and burned before you, your head severed from your body and your body divided into four quarters to be disposed of at the King's pleasure.

A skilled executioner could keep his victim alive until most of his internal organs had been removed and burnt in the brazier placed by his side. The excruciating pain would not have been numbed by the partial asphyxiation brought about by the hanging. If the executioner took pity on him the prisoner may have been allowed to be hanged until almost dead; however, if the crime had been a blatant attempt at rebellion, or the executioner took it upon himself to be cruel and sadistic, the hanging would last only a few seconds at most. The longer the hanging was allowed to continue, the less pain the prisoner would feel as the blades cut through the flesh. After disembowelling the perpetrator, the head would then be cut off and the remaining part of the body split into four quarters. Each of the parts, including the head, would be par-boiled to preserve them, placed on poles and put on display in various parts of the city to forewarn others of the same fate awaiting them following wrong-doings.

In 1538, during the Dissolution of the Monasteries, William Gylham, a monk from Lenton Priory, and four labourers were tried and found guilty of treason. Their sentence of hanging, drawing and quartering was carried out in Nottingham, possibly in the market place. There are two entries in the accounts of 1537-38 making reference to the incident, the first one shows that the town gave the judges two gallons of wine at a cost of 16d, while the second entry says 2d was paid for the clearing of Cow Lane, 'when the monks of Lenton suffered death'. Cow Lane was the name of one of the roads leading to the market place.

Burned at the Stake

The Saxons used burning at the stake as punishment for certain crimes, however, it is perhaps best remembered as the preferred method of despatching alleged witches and religious heretics. A little less well-known is that it was also the legal way of ending the lives of women convicted of high treason and petty treason. It was considered that the male form of execution for high treason (hanging, drawing and quartering) was inappropriate for women, so, in order to preserve their decency from exposing their bodies to public gaze and to save them from having to endure disembowelment in front of a baying crowd, they were to be burned alive instead.

Petty treason was introduced in the Treason Act of 1351, and was defined as; the murder of a husband by his wife, the killing of an ecclesiastic by someone his junior, or the killing of a master by his servant. Women convicted of petty treason were burned at the stake while men were hanged and quartered. In later years, it became customary for the executioner to pass a rope around the woman's neck as she stood tied to the stake and, standing outside the flames as they started to reach higher, he would strangle her so that she would not suffer unduly from the heat and flames.

The only record of anybody being burned at the stake in Nottinghamshire comes from 1575, but no details about the convicted or their crime are known.

Petty treason was abolished in 1828 when the crimes it covered became indistinct from that of murder.

Beheading

Traditionally, the method of ridding the country of unwanted, troublesome aristocrat ne'er-do-wells (depending on your point of view of course) beheading was viewed as a more noble way to depart this world. The spectacle of public execution at the end of a rope was seen to be far too a lowly end to the life of anyone with rank or standing and

The reality of burning at the stake.

The head of Jeremiah Brandreth.

beheading was regarded as a cleaner and swifter end. The Romans regarded it as an honourable way to die, however, following the collapse of the Roman Empire it was not re-introduced into law as a punishment until William the Conqueror thought it desirable to re-use it as a way of controlling high ranking members of his nobility. The first to fall foul of the new law was Walthe, Earl of Huntingdon, who lost his head to the axe man in 1076.

Despite the best efforts of many of the executioners to send their victims into the next world with a single blow, it seldom happened that way. The axe was usually heavy and cumbersome to wield with ease and the thick edge was seldom truly sharp, making the passage through the prisoner's neck none too easy. Instead of a quick and painless death with a single stroke, the dull blade bludgeoned its way through flesh, sinews and bone with up to seven or more blows. Occasionally, one blow was indeed sufficient to end the prisoner's plight but not always.

The last Nottinghamshire man to be beheaded was Jeremiah Brandreth from Wilford, Nottingham. Born in 1790, Brandreth moved to Sutton in Ashfield and is thought to have taken part in the 1811 Luddite riots. By May 1817, Brandreth was out of work and became caught in the government-engineered plot to start a rebellion when he met William Oliver – a government spy and agent provocateur, who convinced him that change was possible with the help of Radicals who were planning an uprising.

On 9 June, Brandreth and 300 followers set off from Pentrich, Derbyshire on a march to Nottingham, when they were intercepted by soldiers near Kimberley. Thirty-five of those captured were tried for High Treason, eleven of whom were transported to Australia for life, while the three ringleaders, Jeremiah Brandreth, William Turner and Isaac Ludlam, were sentenced to be hanged, drawn and quartered. The sentence was later commuted to hanging and beheading.

In November, all three men were hanged in Derby. Their bodies were brought down and their heads removed with an axe. Lifting the head of Brandreth up by the hair the executioner exclaimed, 'Behold the head of a traitor, Jeremiah Brandreth.' Not only was Jeremiah Brandreth the last man from Nottinghamshire to be beheaded, he was also among the last three men ever to be beheaded in England with an axe.

The Last Nottinghamshire Hangmen

The last men from Nottinghamshire to take up the post of Public executioner were Henry Albert Pierrepoint (1878-1922) and his older brother, Thomas William Pierrepoint (1870-1954). The younger brother Henry, a one time butcher's apprentice, was born at

Normanton-on-Soar, the fourth child of Mary and Thomas Pierrepoint, but it was his fascination with the gruesome post of hangman that led him to apply to the Home Office for an official post. In 1901, his wish was granted and he began to assist in the execution of convicted murderers before becoming principal executioner himself. During his term of office he diligently kept a notebook containing the name, weight and height of those he was to hang. This would help him to calculate the length of drop to ensure a quick and clean death for the prisoner. His nine-year tenure of the post of executioner came to an end in July 1910, when he turned up drunk the day before the execution of Frederick Foreman in Chelmsford prison. Described as being 'considerably the worse for drink', it was also alleged that he fought with his assistant, John Ellis. Over the nine-year period he held office, Henry Pierrepoint hanged 105 convicts.

Thomas Pierrepoint, born in Sutton Bonington, was encouraged to enter into the profession by Henry in the name of tradition, claiming Henry taught his older brother the art of hangman by practicing in a stable using sacks of corn and a rope. His forty-year career was not without its problems; as his age began to take hold, doubts were expressed about his ability to perform his duties correctly, and, between 1942 and 1944, he was the subject of an investigation. It was not until the war had finished that he retired in 1946 at the age of seventy-six. During his time as executioner, he despatched nearly 300 prisoners – including a number of US military personnel found guilty of murder and rape (at that time a capital crime under US military law). Thomas died in 1954, thirty-two years after his younger brother Henry, who had died in 1922 aged just forty-four.

—Four—

PUNISHING THE DEAD

Strange as it may seem, there were actually laws in place at one time to punish the dead, and, as a consequence of these laws, it was intended that the dead person's soul could not take its place in heaven. Some of these poor people had not broken any laws of the land but had only transgressed religious beliefs and doctrines – yet still their bodies were treated in a similar way to convicted felons.

The life of a convict had always been considered less worthy than that of a God-fearing, law-abiding citizen, and it was during the reign of Henry VIII that barber-surgeons were given permission to receive the bodies of four convicted and executed criminals per year, for the purpose of dissection. The lack of bodies suitable for medical examination meant that throughout the years demand always far outstretched supply. Over the succeeding centuries, the number of convicts' bodies given over to medical science increased, and yet even this modest rise in supply was not enough. The crime of murder was, quite rightly, seen as the most heinous of crimes and, in an attempt to stifle the alarming rate of killings, the 1752 Murder Act was introduced. Its primary functions were 'for better preventing the horrid crime of murder' by making the consequences of carrying out the act so abhorrent that the potential killer would be dissuaded from their evil course. The shame attached to the death sentence and the subsequent punishment their dead body would receive was believed to be the catalyst for this supposed change in outlook. Anyone found guilty of murder not only suffered the long process of being hanged, but afterwards their body would either be 'dissected and anatomised' or hung in chains as a warning to others. The increase in ready bodies for the medical profession also went part of the way in helping to alleviate the growing problem of grave-robbers.

James Wogden became Nottinghamshire's first criminal to be dissected when he was hanged on 4 April 1752 for murdering Edward Whatman near Ollerton. Once hanged, the body of the convict would be taken back to the doctors for dissection whereupon as many medical practitioners as possible, notable gentry and the plain curious members of the public, would squeeze into the dissection room and watch with glee and anticipation. Once the autopsy had finished, the bones would be boiled and wired together to make a complete skeleton for doctors and students to examine, individual organs would be pickled in jars to preserve them, and in some particularly gruesome cases the skin of the dead was tanned and used as the covers for books and other such items. It was not unknown for members of the public to be allowed to file past the dissected cadaver and the body parts as they were neatly laid out on a table before everything was tidied away.

John Hemstock

In March 1815, John Hemstock stood in the dock accused of the brutal murder of a boy called James Snell. It was alleged that Hemstock (19), in gainful employment on a farm at Clarborough, had clubbed his victim around the head with a piece of wood and had then cut his throat with a razor. Found guilty, he was sentenced to be hanged and anatomised. Following his hanging on 23 March, while still fresh, his body was immediately taken to the general hospital where it was dissected and examined. His bones were boiled and wired together and his skeleton was used in the hospital for many years as an item of display and a teaching aid.

Gibbeting

Gibbeting, or hanging in chains as it was also called, was the alternative use for the body of the murderers following execution. Once hanged, the body would be cut down and covered in tar and canvas (in order to protect the body from decomposition), placed in an iron frame or chains and put on display on a 30ft-high pole – close to where the crime took place. To add to the distress of the prisoner, the blacksmith would measure up the condemned for his chains before the hanging took place. A gibbeting was a relatively rare occurrence and the novelty of such an event would inevitably lead to huge crowds gathering at the gibbet site to watch. Market traders would set up their stalls and sightseers would turn up in their droves. The spectacle of seeing a body swinging in the wind

A depiction of dissection by Hogarth.

Resurrection men at work.

inevitably brought out day trippers and families often came along with picnics to enjoy the day. To stop mischief-makers, nails were driven into the gibbet post to make climbing it harder, and to ensure its durability the post was preserved with tar. Given the chance, any visitors or tourists would take the opportunity to pinch a small slither of the gibbet because it was believed it would ward off or cure toothache.

Robert Downe, aka Robin Down, suffered the ignominy of gibbeting in August 1767 following his conviction for murder. This slow-witted busker from Eckington, Derbyshire was travelling through Mansfield when he was tormented by a number of children. Losing his patience, he chased after the group while brandishing his knife. Catching up with one of the boys, he stabbed him. The unfortunate deaf and mute child, who took the brunt of Downe's anger, died almost instantly and Downe was arrested. Before his trial, the judge decided to check Downe's mental capacity by giving him a test. Placing in front of him a silver coin and a gold coin, the judge asked Downe to choose one; Downe chose the shinier gold coin. The judge decided that he had chosen the gold coin not because it was prettier and shinier, but because it was more valuable, and he thus concluded he was mentally fit to stand trial. After his subsequent execution, Downe's body was gibbeted at Mansfield forest close to where the crime had taken place.

The Hand of Glory

One of the greatest prizes a thief or burglar could obtain was the hand of a newly-executed prisoner in the belief that their 'Hand of Glory' would assist them as they carried out their robberies. If the prisoner had been a murderer the hand that had done the wicked deed was favoured, in all other cases the left hand was the required limb. Once the appendage had been severed from the body and spirited away, it was dried and pickled to preserve it before finally a candle was added to use in the future for illumination. Even the candle had to be made from special ingredients – a mixture of body fat from the executed felon was mixed with virgin wax and Lapland sesame seed oil.

When completed, the burglar took the now magical hand to each burglary, safe in the knowledge that the light from the candle would render him invisible to everyone else or make any witness incapable of moving. As a happy by-product, the hapless burglar was reassured to know the candle could only be extinguished by throwing milk on the flame.

One of the more sought after parts of a gibbeted body was the skull. Once nature had taken its course and decay had set in, eager trophy hunters did their utmost to retrieve the skull, believing that taking a drink from it would cure epilepsy. When it became time to finally remove the gibbet, it was quite common to find some or most of the body missing. Sick people who hoped to find cures for their ailments and trophy hunters made sure there was little that needed burial.

The Resurrection Men

The ready supply of convicts' bodies for dissection still did not fulfil the demand created by an ever-inquisitive medical profession, and the situation became more fraught when the availability of criminals' remains disappeared in 1832. The relevant part of the Murder Act that allowed it (the abolition of gibbeting followed in 1834) was abolished. Grave robbers – the Resurrection Men – now had a greater chance to make some money. As lucrative as the new situation was, grave robbing was already well practiced in the county.

A public outcry engulfed Nottingham in 1827, when one of Pickford's agents became concerned about the contents of a hamper he had been entrusted with in the warehouse. Closer examination revealed two bodies destined for London, and the enquiry that followed discovered a man by the name of Smith living in Maiden lane, along with two partners in crime who were grave robbers. Distressed relatives of newly buried family members flooded into St Mary's graveyard to see if their loved ones were still there, only to find that thirty bodies had been stolen. The irate crowd sought out William Davis, St Mary's gravedigger, and set about him believing he was involved. Guilty or not, Davis barely managed to get away with his life while the real resurrection men escaped.

Felo De Se

Over the years, the act of taking one's own life has gone under a number of different names – suicide, self-murder and *felo de se* (felon of himself), but whatever the title attached to it, until relatively recent time,s the intended 'victim' was virtually guaranteed to get their wish because *felo de se* was a capital offence. If an attempt failed, the survivor was prosecuted and sentenced to death. On the other hand, if the attempt was successful, justice had to be seen to be done so the dead person's body was punished. Until 1823, anyone taking their own life knew that their body would not be buried on consecrated ground within a churchyard – instead it was taken to a crossroads and buried by the roadside in the belief that, should the suicide victims soul manage to rise from the earth, it would not know which road to take on its journey back to its home. As an added twist, a wooden stake was driven through the corpse to show that it had not escaped the death penalty.

One of the sites in Nottingham that these unfortunates were interred now lies beneath Derby Road. Originally known as the Sandhills, this open crossroads was the scene of a number of burials when, in 1764, John Higgins was buried after he hanged himself with his lovers handkerchief, followed eight years later by Thomas Smith and latterly in 1800 by John Caunt, aka George Caunt.

Caunt, a hairdresser of St James' Street, Nottingham was accused of the theft of a pair of curtains. Fearing the consequences of capture and transportation – or worse, the death penalty – he escaped capture by taking refuge in a friend's house. Keeping watch, but not attempting to storm the house, the police satisfied themselves by keeping Caunt a virtual prisoner within the house. In the end, Caunt's patience gave out; arming himself with a pistol, he ran out of the house, whereupon a constable leapt on him and attempted to disarm him. A shot rang out, and, in the ensuing confusion, Caunt escaped, leaving behind the wounded constable. Making his way to Alfreton, Caunt was at last captured but still he was able to avoid being sent to trial when he managed to take poison. The coroner's inquest passed the verdict of *felo de se* and his body was interred at the crossroads. It was his friends who were to have the final say when they dug up his body and had it reburied in the Baptist cemetery on Stoney Street.

Not everyone who took their own life suffered the full vent of the law. When Thomas Morris took his own life in 1787, he was given the privilege of being buried in a coffin. Perhaps Morris' standing in the community as Nottingham's first Sunday school teacher evoked a sympathetic reaction.

The practice of crossroads burials continued until 1823 when the law was changed to allow victims of *felo de se* to be buried within the confines of a graveyard, provided the interment took place between the hours of 9 p.m. and midnight. No clergy were allowed to perform a ceremony and a true Christian burial was prohibited, including the refusal to allow the burial to be entered into the parish register.

Inquest juries did their utmost to find the cause of a person's death, and, when it was obvious that the dead person they were investigating had taken their own life, they often attributed the cause to 'temporary insanity'. This permitted any relatives to give their loved ones a formal burial. Seldom was a verdict of *felo de se* passed but on the odd occasion it was, it was done with great reluctance in the full knowledge of the consequences.

The Reverend William Brown

In November 1848, an inquest held in the Gate public house Nottingham was given the task of deciding why the Reverend William Brown had taken his own life. The twenty-five-year-old curate from Sneinton had taken a fancy to the seventeen-year-old daughter of another clergyman, Revd Edward Bull, and, deciding to take the honourable course, Brown informed Bull of his feelings towards the girl. Revd Bull thought his daughter too young for such a relationship and informed Brown of his thoughts in a letter. As soon as Brown had read the note, he immediately went out and bought a pistol along with ammunition. Without any apparent hesitation, he then went into Nottingham Castle yard and shot himself. When his body was found and his pockets were searched, the letter from the Revd Bull was discovered. The inquest jury passed a verdict of temporary insanity and William Brown received a Christian burial.

A Consequence of Taking Arsenic

Ann Frisby was a servant working for Joseph Payne, a farmer of Widmerpool who, in April 1838, took her own life to end her troubles. The nineteen-year-old woman's death caused quite a stir at the inquest and a large number of witnesses were called to give evidence. The two surgeons, who examined Ann's body, discovered she had died from arsenic poisoning and, more surprisingly, that she was approximately one month pregnant. Suspicion for supplying the poison fell on the son of a well-respected local man, and it was also implied that the son might well have administered the deadly drug to Ann. At the very least, he was thought to have known about Ann's intentions. After a great deal of deliberation, the jury returned a verdict of 'Died as a consequence of taking a dose of arsenic whilst labouring under a temporary fit of insanity'.

Try as they might, the juries at inquests could not always pass the verdict of insanity and, reluctantly, they sometimes felt forced to conclude the only outcome had to be *felo de se*.

The body of Martha King was found in the well of the Green Dragon on Long Row, Nottingham in February 1765, and suspicion for her death immediately fell onto a soldier she had been keeping close company with. Martha had been missing for four or five days and the discovery of her body must have caused quite a stir. Close examination of the soldier showed he had not been the cause of Martha's demise and the jury passed the verdict of *felo de se*.

Fined for Giving a Good Send Off

Sometimes it was not the dead that were punished but, instead, it was those who gave them a good send off. On 18 July 1656, the good people of Misterton were fined £10 for allowing the burial of an illegitimate child before the coroner could hold an inquest. It was suspected that the child had been 'made away'.

The Terrible Tale of John Spencer

British justice can, at times, come across as being slow and cumbersome, while in other instances its speed can be surprising. Take the case of John Spencer, whose date with destiny was swift and his punishment long.

Just north of Scrooby lay one of the Great North Road's turnpikes, and on 2 July 1779, John Spencer concluded he would have the takings kept inside for himself – after all he had debts and this would be a good way of ridding himself of that burden. Between seven and eight in the evening, he made his way to the toll house and engaged William Yeadon, the toll keeper, and his mother Mary in conversation. Staying till about nine, he then excused himself and wandered around the common until he was sure no-one else was around. At around two in the morning of 3 July, when he was confident he was alone, Spencer went to the toll bar and called William Yeadon out, claiming he had some beasts that he wanted to take through. As soon as Yeadon appeared, Spencer knocked him over with a hedge stake and then rained blows down mercilessly on the defenceless mans head.

A broadsheet telling the story of John Spencer. (Nottingham Local Studies Library)

Gibbet Hill, Scrooby, where John Spencer's body was gibbeted.

A grim reminder at Scrooby — Gibbet Hill Lane.

Believing his victim to be dead, Spencer then went inside the toll house and took a watch off of the 'chimney piece' before making his way upstairs. Spotting Mary Yeadon asleep in bed, he once more raised the hedge stake in a menacing manner before striking her over the head. Thinking that he was leaving behind two dead people, he ran out of the house and made his escape.

The following morning, two waggoners arriving at the toll bar were horrified to find William Yeadon sprawled on the ground – horribly injured, but still alive. Alerted to the tragedy, the villagers of Scrooby came out to give any help they could and it was then that they found William Yeadon was still breathing. A quick search of the toll house soon led to the discovery of Yeadon's dead mother lying in her blood-soaked bed. The surgeon who attended Yeadon found that his skull had been fractured in two places. Despite his best efforts, William Yeadon died two days later without ever being able to speak. It looked as if Spencer had managed to get away with murder after all.

As the murders were taking place, a Mr Newcomb was detained in Retford on business, and, while there, heard of the Scrooby killings and the missing watch. Newcomb's return to his home in Gainsborough brought a surprising turn of events when his maid told of how a local shoemaker had bought a watch from a stranger the day before. With his suspicions aroused, Newcomb followed the trail of the watch to the shoe maker and bought it for a guinea, then, after gaining a description of the stranger from those who had seen him, he made his way to Scrooby, where the watch was identified as William Yeadon's. Satisfied that his initial thoughts about the watch had been correct, Newcomb informed the local authorities, who reasoned from the description he supplied, that the stranger who had originally sold the watch was John Spencer. Newcomb, Mr Diamond, and three others set off to Willoughton, where Spencer was believed to be living, and managed to apprehend the suspect.

Though he initially denied the charge, Spencer later admitted to stealing the watch; the murder, however, he laid at the feet of his alleged accomplice – a local wrongdoer. The new suspect was arrested and questioned intensely, but it soon become clear that Spencer had lied again, when the wrongdoer was able to prove he had been asleep in a village miles away from Scrooby at the time of the murders.

Content that there was enough evidence for a prosecution, Spencer was sent for trial, nonetheless, throughout his trial and the lead up to it he constantly maintained that he was not the killer and had only stolen the watch. Evidence at the scene of the murder and in the nearby fields confirmed Spencer's story about how he had entered the toll house, but crucially it did not confirm he was accompanied by anyone.

In a trial lasting four hours, the damning evidence was aired in court, and, when it became time for the jury to deliberate, they made their decision in just two minutes – guilty. The judge passed the only sentence available for such a crime when he sentenced Spencer to be hanged and his body to be gibbeted, but not dissected. Gibbeting and dissecting were not a formal part of the death sentence, but, once executed, the body of a criminal was forfeit to the state and could be disposed of as seen fit under the 1742 Murder Act.

John Spencer was hanged in Nottingham on 26 July 1779, just twenty-three days after committing a double murder; he had no chance of an appeal or having the sentence commuted. Once he had been hanged, his body was cut down, covered in tar and canvas to preserve it and finally placed in an iron cage so that it could be suspended from a high wooden pole. Transported to Scrooby, Spencer's body was hauled up high onto the gibbet post on Gibbet Hill, close to the toll house, to act as a warning to others. As a final reminder of the tragic episode that had taken place there just weeks earlier, the hedge stake, that had been used as the weapon of murder, was placed in the dead man's hand.

The weeks passed by and the sight of Spencer's lifeless corpse swinging in the breeze became less of a distraction, until a group of soldiers escorting a deserter came across the spectacle. Taking his carbine, the sergeant in charge discharged his weapon into Spencer's body – the ball piercing the tar and canvas and allowing decay and rot to set in. Over the coming days and weeks, the decomposing body gave out a dreadful smell that caused 'a pestilential odour over Scrooby'. The group of soldiers were followed and the sergeant was reported for his actions. At his subsequent court-martial, he was reduced to the ranks for wasting ammunition.

The gibbet proved such an attraction that on many Sundays, families came out and held picnics beneath the body and hawkers and tradesmen plied their goods to any willing buyer and needless to say souvenir collectors also turned up in the hope of acquiring some memento.

The years rolled by and Spencer's body gradually decomposed until at last there was nothing left. When trophy hunters and nature had had their way, only the cage was left and then even that fell down and was spirited away. The gibbet post finally toppled on 15 April 1846, nearly sixty-seven years after it was first erected, except that was not the end of the gibbet post, part of which was clearly seen in a nearby field being used as a gatepost with the date 1779 carved into it as a reminder of the dreadful affair that took place all those years ago.

The Deodand

For many centuries, the laws of Deodand were used to blame an animal or inanimate object which had caused the death of a human being, to ensure that some form of punishment could be apportioned to the bringer of death. Derived from the term *Deo dandum*, 'to be given to God', it gave the coroner's courts power to confiscate the offending object and give it to the monarch or Church to be sold and the money accrued was to be put to pious uses. In later years, the coroner's court simply placed a value on the object and took the funds from the owner of the murderous article.

When the inquest on the death of John Allsop was held at the Salutation pub, in Keyworth on 1 July 1835, the jury heard how he had been oiling the workings of the windmill, in which he was working, and had slipped into the cogs and gears. His rescuers found he had crushed his neck, face and right hand and, despite their best efforts, he died later that day. The jury placed a deodand of 6d on the machinery that had killed Allsop.

Almost seven years later, on 6 June 1842, an inquest jury heard the tragic story of Eliza Hind who had been killed three days earlier at Radford. Poor Eliza had been standing next to the river that ran opposite her house when a cart came by. The young boy driving the cart was taken by surprise when the horse suddenly turned towards the river to get a drink, taking both of them dangerously close to Eliza. One of the wheels of the cart caught Eliza and tossed her into a wall, where her head crashed against a cornerstone, causing fatal injuries. After a deliberation, the jury returned a verdict that Eliza had died 'as a consequence of being accidentally run over by a mare and cart' with a deodand of £5 placed on both the mare and cart.

The laws of Deodand were abolished on 1 September 1846; following a series of terrible train crashes, the government questioned whether some of the blame for accidents should be apportioned away from the object causing death onto the shoulders of those responsible for operating the killing article. One train crash near Beeston station late in 1844, between two trains belonging to the Midland Railway, resulted in the death of two people and the injury of many more. At the inquest of William Varnells, one of the victims of the crash, the jury heard all the evidence and deliberated for many hours before arriving at a verdict in which they did not assign any blame to the Midland Railway or its employees, instead they found the guilt for the crash fell '[…] upon the engine, tenders and carriages [...]' In consequence, they imposed a deodand of £1,000 on the offending trains.

—Five—

SOCIAL STRIFE

In 1789, the American Benjamin Franklyn wrote a letter to a friend, in which he said 'In this world nothing can be said to be certain, except death and taxes'. Perhaps he should have also included in that letter the blight of noisy neighbours, dodgy workmen and making mistakes. Some of the social difficulties that ran through Nottinghamshire were deep-rooted and caused a great deal of misery and hardship, often culminating with civil disorder that led to riots and, in some cases, an eventual change in the law. Other problems were brought about by government policy and working condition, but, for as long as there have been laws, someone, somewhere has been breaking them – either deliberately or through ignorance, and some of the problems that have cropped up over the centuries seem to be the same old ones.

At a hearing in Nottingham in 1518, Robert Mellors prosecuted Thomas Blythe of Linby, for failing to keep an agreement from five years earlier in which Blythe had agreed to build Mellors a house. Thankful for a successful outcome, Mellors was pleased to discover that Thomas Blythe was ordered to pay £20 in damages.

The menace of the cowboy builder has lurked in the background since builders have first been employed and the court records have numerous cases whereby builders and masons have left jobs unfinished. In July 1637, a mason from Annesley Woodhouse was presented at court for 'not making an end of work' and William Berridge had to do some quick thinking in 1689 when he stood in the dock accused of 'not erecting a building according to a contract with John Sturtivant'. Whether they had to finish the work or another builder was employed is open to question.

Parish's found that they could not escape the wrath of the courthouse if they failed to do their civic duties either. Over the years, each parish gained more and more responsibility for looking after the needs of the local infrastructure, as well as assuring tradesmen and women adhered to the law, and it could come as a severe financial shock if the courts ordered the Parish to carry out any repairs to the roads, or anything else it was held responsible for. In 1553, Queen Mary passed a law that the parishes were responsible for maintaining the road and, by law, all inhabitants of a village had to give their time free of charge to repair them, and if they could not do the work themselves they had to ensure a replacement worker turned out.

When the people of Lenton and Wollaton declined to take part in looking after the roads in their own parishes, they were each fined 1s, and the people of Halam had to pay 10s to the Overseers of the Highways when they just failed to turn up for work.

There was no avoiding responsibility for those in charge either, when the Surveyors of Misterton were indicted in 1640 for failing to tell the inhabitants of the village that they had to spend six days repairing the roads.

The repair of bridges was a constant source of discontent among local parishes, when they could not agree whose responsibility it was to keep them in a good state. Many cases were brought to trial, as each of the parties denied liability for looking after each of these bridges. In the late seventeenth century, the County of Nottingham suffered a huge defeat in court when they had to defend themselves over the poor condition of the bridge at Trowell. The judge ruled that the county must raise £50 to repair the bridge and a further £2 to pay their defence attorney, Francis Haynes.

Taxes, then as now, were a bone of contention and it was not unknown for the collectors of the taxes to supplement their income by helping themselves to some of the taxes they had gathered. In 1340, the taxmen lined their own pockets when they took 12s from the citizens of Balderton and kept it for themselves instead of donating it to the King.

The whole gambit of social order and disorder has played its part over time in shaping today's society – but not all the men and women that broke the law realised just what they were doing wrong, as William Ball found out as he took his place in court in January 1873.

Arrested and charged with obstruction, by Inspector Christopher Hopkinson, as he walked down Lister Gate in Nottingham, Ball was quickly found guilty and fined 10s – his crime was to be caught carrying a bag of soot down the causeway (Ball was a chimney sweep).

Riot and Affray

For some strange reason, Nottinghamshire has been one of the main focal points for public anger and uprisings against governments for hundreds of years. Perhaps the image of Robin Hood fighting against the evil Sheriff of Nottingham influenced people into believing that actions speak louder than words. In 1811, the Luddite riots began when the followers of the possibly imaginary Ned Ludd began an eight-year fight against mechanisation in the textile industry. Ludd, who was said to live in Sherwood Forest, became the infamous leader of the Luddites, as gangs of workers smashed the new machinery they believed was taking away their livelihood. Civil unrest spread as far as Derbyshire, Leicestershire, Yorkshire and Lancashire, with sporadic outbreaks of violence and machinery breaking. In Nottinghamshire, many mill owners, parish overseers and town authorities took the threat seriously enough to employ armed watchmen and to use the militia when necessary.

In June 1812, the overseers at Hucknall paid the Nottingham Magistrates Clerk, Mr Sculthorpe £510 for supplying firearms, while at the same time paying for fourteen watchmen – Ben Walker receiving the princely sum of 2s for each night.

If caught and found guilty, the Luddites could expect swift and harsh justice; Ben Hancock of Hucknall learnt this first-hand when he was transported to Australia in 1812 for fourteen years after being convicted of breaking machinery at Sutton. George Green, also from Hucknall, was transported for seven years. Green must have realised that life in

Australia was preferable to that back in England because once his sentence was finished he decided to stay on and continue with his new life.

Unrest once more came to Nottingham in 1831 with the Reform Bill riots, a huge public outburst of frustration and anger. In March, over 9,000 people had signed a petition in favour of reform, but when the bill was rejected in October the news was met with horror. The Whig government, under Earl Grey, had passed the Reform Bill, a proposal to reform Parliament and designed to eliminate some of the unfairness in the voting system. However, the Tory-led House of Lords threw the bill out and the seeds of unrest had been set. All over the country, violence broke out with some of the most intense being in Nottingham.

Trouble started on 9 October, when reformers targeted the homes of anti-reformers – causing the Mayor to call in the constables to try to regain control of the situation after he had read the Riot Act. The following day, an angry group made their way to Colwick Hall, and, after forcing entry, they ransacked it before setting fire to a part of it. The group's next target was Nottingham Castle, where once more the group forced their way in to cause damage. With the Duke of Newcastle away from the castle, the mob set fire to it and soon it was a blazing inferno. Their next target was a silk mill in Beeston, which was also set alight and burned down.

Retribution swiftly followed and George Beck, George Hearson and John Armstrong were soon arrested for the burning of the mill. Beck, from Wollaton, Hearson, from Nottingham and Armstrong from Pleasley, (Derbys) were all hanged on 1 February 1832.

Out of all the prosecutions that followed the three days of rioting, perhaps the greatest miscarriage of justice was against the seventeen-year-old Valentine Marshall, a framework knitter from Coal Pit Lane. At his trial in the Shire Hall, a number of witnesses testified he had been present at the burning of Colwick Hall – yet there were other witnesses who claimed he was elsewhere at the time. Possibly under pressure, the jury found Marshall guilty and he was sentenced to be hanged, this was later commuted to transportation to Australia for life.

After a brief stay in gaol and a spell on the hulk ship *Justitia* at Woolwich, Marshall was sent to Van Diemen's Land (Tasmania) where he settled down to a new life and gained a free pardon in 1842, a rarity amongst lifer's who traditionally could only earn a conditional pardon. Despite saying he would return to England he never did, preferring to stay in his new homeland.

The Problem with Bread and Ale

King Henry III shocked the bakery and brewery trades in 1266, when he introduced the Assize of Bread and Ale, which laid down strict regulations on the manufacturing, quality, weight and price of bread and ale. Any unfortunate brewers, bakers or tradesman who broke any of the regulations could be fined, placed in the pillory or flogged. It was the fear of being accused of selling short measures that induced bakers to make the dozen consist of thirteen and not twelve loaves.

Presented before the court in April 1642, Edward Hooton was charged with brewing without a licence and keeping a disorderly house during Sunday service. Unable to pay his fine, he was whipped in front of the constable the following Sunday.

The first changes to the Assize of Bread and Ale did not come until 1822, with more amendments in 1836 and its final abolition in 1863.

Bull-Baiting

It was a long held belief that the baiting of bulls would make the meat tastier, tender and more palatable, and for centuries many towns and villages had an iron ring fixed into the ground, or to a strong post, to which the bull was tied before trained dogs were set upon it. The practice was eventually abolished in 1835, but, until then, bull-baiting was a serious occasion and failure to follow strict protocol would lead to prosecution.

On 16 November 1584, Robert Cave, William Brasse and William Blythe of Tuxford admitted that they had been bull-baiting on the Sabbath but not, as the prosecution claimed, during service time. For their pains, all three were told to put 1s each into the poor box.

It was regarded as an important part of village and town life to take care of any commonly owned livestock. In 1687, four men from Gedling were presented for not looking after the 'towne bull' for the space of thirteen weeks as instructed.

As common and open as bull-baiting was, not everyone agreed with it and one elderly man in Nottingham, called Leavers, caused a bit of a stir at one such event in the town. During the fight between the bull and the dogs, the bull got the upper hand with one dog, tossing it high in the air only to land at Leaver's feet. The furious owner of the dog shouted at Leavers, telling him should have caught the dog as the rules of baiting said. Leavers calmly replied that he wanted the bull to win.

An ale and beer notice.

Newark market place bull baiting post.

Witches and Witchfinders

The fear of witchcraft and sorcery had driven Henry VIII to introduce the Witchcraft Act of 1541, making witchcraft punishable by death, but, under Elizabeth I, the offence attracted the less severe punishment of imprisonment – unless the sorcery had inflicted harm upon the victim, and the death penalty was to be given.

With the accession of James I to the throne in 1603, a new witchcraft law soon followed when An Act Against Conjuration, Witchcraft and dealing with evil and wicked spirits came in 1604. Under the new ruling, anyone convicted of a serious act of witchcraft was hanged, unless found guilty of witchcraft involving petty treason (the harming of a superior), in which case the offender was burnt at the stake. Those convicted of lesser offences were sentenced to one year in prison; second offences resulted in the death penalty.

Changing attitudes meant that, by 1735, when a new Witchcraft Act was enacted, witchcraft had all but been dismissed as a fallacy, and the new law concentrated on making the pretence of witchcraft illegal. For almost two centuries, to be accused of indulging in the supposed darker side of life could have brought about harsh punishments. Not all judges took the evidence at face value, and many cases were dismissed out of hand.

On 24 April 1583, Widow Wright stood trial suspected of sorcery. She had been accused by a prisoner at his own execution. Although the widow pleaded not guilty, the judge ordered her to do Penance, quite probably just to be on the safe side. In 1616, a warrant was issued against Christian Clark, Elizabeth Hudson and Susan Hudson of North Muskham for using incantations against Anna Strey – unfortunately the outcome of their trial is not known.

Mansfield-born witch finder John Darrell came to notoriety in 1598, when he was shown to be fraudulent. Following the sensational exorcism of a girl in Derbyshire, Darrell was appointed curate to St Mary's church in Nottingham, where he claimed he knew of thirteen witches in the town. At the exorcism of a boy called William Somers, Darrell claimed the boy's violent fits were a sign of the devil, and, when the boy started to give the names of so called witches, panic spread like wildfire as people tried to distance themselves from the accusations. Somers' sister also started to fit, and suspicions soon began to surface that all was not as it seemed. Close questioning of the boy soon revealed that both he and his sister had been taught by Darrell to act as they did. Darrell was arrested, stripped of his Holy Orders and thrown in prison, where he languished until the following year.

For Sale, One Wife

Many strange things can be sold in a market place, but perhaps none stranger than the sale of a wife. April 1852 saw a Mr Stephenson take his wife into Nottingham market place and put her up for sale. As she stood there with a new rope draped around her neck, he proudly announced that for 2s 6d the buyer not only got his wife, but also the brand new rope. She was eventually sold for 1s but, ironically, when it came to signing the contract of sale, the wife was the only one who could write.

Bastardy

Under successive poor laws, the burden of caring for an unmarried mother and her illegitimate child fell upon the parish from where she originated, often causing a drain on the parish coffers. In an attempt to make both parents face their responsibilities, various measures could be taken to alleviate the problem – including forced marriage, or a judgement obliging the father to make regular payments for the child's upkeep. Other more punitive punishments could, and would, be frequently made to show any potentially wayward fornicators the error of taking the wrong path. On 11 April 1621, both parents of an illegitimate child from Coddington were ordered to be whipped according to the law.

Harsh as this sentence was, the judge could have added a spell in the House of Correction for one year, as authorised in an Act passed in 1609 under James I. Gertrude Stafford of Gamston, found to her cost that she was to spend a year behind bars in January 1652-53, when she was found guilty of 'being a lewd woman' after having several illegitimate children, the last two (twins) dying shortly after birth. Any women sent to gaol for bearing a child out of wedlock would have to take their child with them as they served their sentence.

Trouble in the Workhouse

The origins of the workhouse date back to the early seventeenth century, when individual towns and cities made provision for providing accommodation for the poor and destitute of their parish. The Act for the Relief of the Poor, passed in 1601, under Elizabeth I, obliged the parish to provide work for the destitute but not accommodation, this was to be decided locally and, in the early years, was limited to the possibility of supplying housing. Gradually more formal workhouses began to appear which gave a roof over the heads of some of the poor at least. The burden of financing the schemes fell onto the shoulders of the local property owners, who could not always find enough money to cover all the needs of the poor and so neighbouring parishes, within the same Hundred, could be ordered by the courts to make a contribution. On 14 January 1690, the parishioners of Coddington, Cottam, Hawton and Barnby were instructed that they each had to pay 6d every week to pay for the upkeep of the poor of Balderton.

With the implementation of the Poor Law Amendment Act in 1834, the Poor Law Commission gained powers to gather parishes into Poor Law Unions, each one being run by a Board of Guardians. Nottinghamshire had nine of the new style workhouses, Basford, Bingham, East Retford, Mansfield, Newark, Nottingham, Radford, Southwell and Worksop, with the emphasis now concentrating on keeping out those who were not truly needy. The men, women and children were to be housed separately, even to the detriment of family groups; contact between adults and their children was strictly limited. Married couples seldom had time to see each other privately, and fraternisation was strictly prohibited unless authorised and supervised.

The daily routine was laid down amongst the strict workhouse rules; from the time that they arose in the morning, to the time that they went to bed, the inmates knew exactly what they would be doing and where. Work was issued to all the able bodied to keep them active, both physically and mentally, and to assist in the running and upkeep of the workhouse. On entry, newcomers were given a coarse, hard-wearing, uncomfortable uniform to wear that remained the property of each workhouse and that had to be returned when they left. As strict and regimented as life was, there was still the inevitable unrest as frustrations and differences flared up into anger. James Naylor, a pauper in Basford workhouse, was sent to Southwell House of Correction to do fourteen days' hard labour

The staff of Mansfield Workhouse c.1900. (Mansfield Museum)

Mansfield Workhouse c.1900. (Mansfield Museum)

in October 1850, when he refused to obey the 'lawful commands of Mr Johnson master of the house'.

At Southwell workhouse on 21 October 1852, Eliza Alvey was stopped her porridge at breakfast for neglecting to attend morning prayers, while in March 1876, William Crook was placed in confinement for nine hours and had to make do with bread, instead of dinner and supper, because he used obscene language towards the nurse.

Theft was a constant thorn in the side of the guardians and masters of the workhouses. The most common thefts were not that of valuable items, as one might suspect, purely because very few things of value were kept in workhouses; clothing was thereby top on the wanted list of most thieves. Many of the men and women absconded, taking with them the clothing they had been issued with on entry, bringing with it a charge of theft. At the Worksop workhouse in April 1870, John Collier, a forty-year-old 'casual pauper', hid in a cupboard until the doors were opened in the morning. As soon as he saw his chance to escape, he clambered through a fence and ran away taking with him a spoon, two handkerchiefs and the clothes he stood up in – the workhouse uniform. The police were immediately informed and a search begun which led to his capture at Blythe about seven miles away. Within days, Collier had been up in court charged with theft and sentenced to two months' hard labour.

By no means did everyone who entered into a workhouse regard it as a safe haven, that would keep them warm and fed in a harsh world, as they tried to get their life back on track; a lot of them viewed their situation as akin to being in prison. A quick look at the Southwell workhouse punishment book shows all too clearly how Henry Stanley felt about his predicament, as the numerous entries listing his behaviour show.

—Date—	—Crime—	—Punishment—
8 March 1854	Neglecting to work	8 hours in the refractory ward (sent to prison for 7 days hard labour for breaking the door of the refractory ward)
16 March 1854	Attempting to run away	7 hours in the refractory ward
14 October 1854	Ran away but came back	Overlooked the next day
19 November 1855	Ran away and was found at Markham. Brought back 1lb of stolen potatoes	His regular servings of meat at dinner were stopped.
11 May 1862	Theft of clothes and absconding	Caught by the police and given 7 days' hard labour

The age of the workhouse lasted for over 400 years until the system's demise in 1948, when the welfare state was introduced, but even then the buildings carried on as large numbers of them were put to other uses, a lingering memory of harder times.

Riding the Stang

Riding the Stang, ran-tanning, rough music and rang-tang are all different names for the same neighbourhood-inflicted retribution. If it was discovered that a man ill-treated his wife, the neighbours would gather together and carry pots, pans and anything else that would make a loud noise, and march en-masse to the offending husband's house in the early hours of the morning and make as much noise as they could. Trumpets, penny whistles, buckets,

Ran-Tanning at Rampton c.1907. (NCCN000341 Courtesy of Nottinghamshire County Council and www. picturethepast.org.uk)

tin cans, and anything that could be used to wake even the heaviest sleeper was employed. In their midst would also be a cart with an effigy of the offender prominently displayed in the back to add further humiliation to the, now-wide-awake, culprit.

For three consecutive nights this rag-tag parade would do the rounds until the effigy was burned on the last night. If the wayward husband had been particularly cruel, he would be forcibly put in the back of the cart, along with his effigy, and be taken round the whole village to show him off. The local constable usually turned a blind eye to the raucous uproar taking place as he turned over and went back to sleep. The last case of riding the stang to take place in Nottinghamshire occurred in Rampton in 1907, when the offender locked himself away and refused to come out.

Plague and Pestilence

The fear that the plague brought in its wake led to all manner of changes in society in an effort to avoid the death and destruction that seemed to follow closely behind it. The doctors and physicians of the time knew that there were thirty-three possible symptoms of the disease, but no cure was known to work. To avoid being infected, all sorts of precautions were taken. In 1604, the Newark Quarter Sessions were moved to Rolston, and, in 1611, the Nottingham Sessions were held in Burton Joyce to evade the disease. Not everyone who caught the plague died, and a great many of those infected made a good recovery, but the seventeenth century was perhaps the peak for the plague in England, and a large number of laws were introduced to suppress its effect. In October 1637, four apparently healthy men from Bingham were prosecuted for playing an illegal game of football 'being or lately affected with the plague'.

At the Rolston Sessions in 1604, the court gave an order that the county must pay Newark £10 per week for one month, so that they could cover the charges for night watchmen to keep the infected in their houses and the healthy out – in effect a forced quarantine.

New rules were brought in to force the Hundreds to pay a levy to help relieve their neighbours, who were being ravaged by the plague and, in January 1637, the Hundreds of Broxtowe, Rushcliffe and Bingham were each ordered to pay 5 Marks in rotation for three weeks to the inhabitants of Radford.

To stop the spread of the plague, numerous people were prosecuted for touching items associated with the illness. A butcher from Norwell was prosecuted in April 1627 for 'killing meat infected with plague' while in January 1637, Anne Smith of West Bridgford, had a warrant issued against her for taking clothes from a plague-infected house.

Newark and the north of the county suffered one last big outbreak of the disease in 1666, when a curious incident happened in Holme. Nan Scott was so fearful of the plague that she stored a huge amount of food in a room over the porch of the church, so that she could safely take refuge if the need arose. When the plague hit, Nan took to her safe place, and, as time passed, she watched as one by one her friends and neighbours were buried. After it looked as though the pestilence had passed, she ventured out only to discover that she and one other were the only ones left. Distraught at finding everyone else was gone, Nan went back to her little room and never came out again.

Settlement and Removal

The 1662 Settlement Act made it compulsory for each person to have a parish of legal settlement, and, under the law, this was the only parish in which they would be entitled to benefit from poor relief in times of hardship. The usual parish to shoulder the responsibility was that of the person's birthplace. However, if the individual in question had lived or worked in another parish for one year or more then that parish became responsible. Each applicant for a settlement order underwent an examination, and, if successful, a Settlement Certificate was issued, which was proof of their entitlement to relief if times were hard.

The burial of plague victims.

Anyone seeking relief without a certificate would be removed to the parish of their settlement, as no-one wanted to carry the expense of caring for strangers who had no right to relief.

At the Nottingham Quarter Sessions of April 1759, Thomas Gelsthorpe managed to get overturned an earlier court ruling that he and his family be removed from Dirty Hucknall (Huthwaite), and sent to Teversal. At the appeal, Chiverton Hartopp and William Bilbie, the two Justices of the Peace, gave permission for Gelsthorpe, his wife Mary and their two children to return to Dirty Hucknall.

Although a poor family, the Gelsthorpe's knew their rights; at the Retford Quarter Sessions of October 1786, Ann Gelsthorpe, the daughter of Thomas and Mary, stood accused of dwelling in the wrong parish while in hardship. Ann had legally moved from Teversal to Blidworth, after being issued with a Settlement Certificate. However, the pauper Ann had decided to move back to Teversal, perhaps to be with her family. When the parish officers found out she was back and about to be a burden on their funds, they applied for a removal order. This time the court backed the parish officers and Ann was removed back to Blidworth.

Plough Monday

The age-old tradition of Plough Monday was, in itself, harmless fun. Farm workers and labourers would dress up all in manner of outrageous costumes and paint their faces, pulling behind them a plough. All the while, they were being driven about the area by a 'drover', who kept them together by hitting them with an inflated bladder tied to the end of a stick. As they travelled around they would shout out, 'Remember the plough bullocks', before asking for a contribution from each household and finishing off the day with a well-earned feed and a large drink at the nearest inn.

Should anyone be foolish enough to refuse to pay up to the happy-go-lucky farmers, they would take great delight in ploughing up the front garden of the offender. Occasionally, the ploughmen took it upon themselves to make their way into the houses of unsuspecting victims, only to find the neighbours piling in to eject them.

One old widow who fell foul to having her garden ploughed up managed to get the ploughmen arrested and put before the magistrate, who made them pay for the damage. They avoided that particular area from then on.

Couvade

Many years ago, men – in the the strong, albeit misguided, belief that they were being a great help– would help their wives while they were in child birth by performing couvade. Instead of busying themselves around the house or helping the midwife, they would, instead, retire to an adjoining room and pretend to go through the full gambit of labour pains in the belief it would lessen their wife's troubles. The only real pain that the man encountered was when his frustrated and unappreciative wife gave him a swift whack if she thought he had been foolish.

-Six-

PRISONS, PRISONERS AND THE POLICE

It was not until the second half of the eighteenth century that prisons began to be built for the long-term imprisonment of offenders. Up until that point, prisons and gaols had been used primarily for short-term confinement while the accused awaited trial, which meant that, for a large part of the time, the cells were underused – towards trial times they were packed to bursting point, with terrible conditions for felons. In the early day's, castles, town halls, guildhalls and many other types of public buildings had their own cells which were normally in poor condition with little or no effort put into the welfare of anyone kept there.

It was during the early 1300s, that the dungeons of Newark castle were used to incarcerate some of the Knight's Templar before they stood trial, after Edward II ordered the suppression of their Order. Nottingham Castle was also used as a gaol when, in 1644, it was used to imprison the Royalist Sir Roger Cooper of Thurgaton and forty of his men, who had been captured by the Parliamentarians. In both of these cases, the prisoners were high profile and their treatment is relatively well-documented for the era in which it took place but, for the majority of those held, their crimes and their final outcomes have gone unrecorded. Imprisonment was the mainstay of keeping undesirables out of the way as more honest folk plied their daily trade. Even during the Tudor period, Nottingham had a gaol underneath the County Hall on High Pavement, and another at the Town Hall – showing the necessity for a formal presence for law and order in the county.

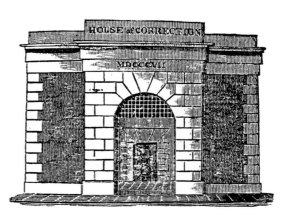

Southwell House of Correction.

Nottingham Guild Hall, 1741.

The use of gaol and incarceration as a deterrent very often failed, as the case of John Shaw goes to show. At the Nottingham Sessions of January 1815, he was convicted of larceny and sentenced to one month's hard labour along with a public whipping. Three months later, at the April Sessions, Shaw was once more found guilty of larceny – this time, however, he was transported to Australia for seven years.

Debt was viewed as a serious offence, and special cells for debtors were added to most prisons specifically for that crime. By the eighteenth century, Nottingham's debtors and felons prisons were both beneath the Guild Hall, but it was the debtors that had the hardest time because they were the only prisoners who were intentionally destined to spend months and years locked away, serving a potentially neverending sentence. Not only did they have to repay any debt before they could be released, just like the rest of the inmates, they also had to pay for their upkeep. They would have to pay the gaoler for any food or drink they consumed and for any comfort that made their life easier, unless – of course – they had a kindly relative or friend willing to help. In 1800, James Neild published details of the conditions that debtors endured in the debtors' prison at the side of the Shire Hall, where the inmates had to pay 3s per week for a bed and bedding, or if two were willing to share a bed they were each charged 2s. The debtor was, however, able to take up paid work to reduce their debt, sometimes being allowed outside the confines of the prison to earn a living, while others had to put any skill they had to use in the prison itself. Begging for alms was considered normal for debtors who had to endure life with the prospect of perpetual incarceration a distinct possibility. By the middle of the nineteenth century the whole prison, in particular the debtors' area, was described as being in a poor state of repair.

Peveril Prison, the debtors gaol at Lenton, seems to have had a more relaxed air about it, with a number of the inmates able to work as waiters and servants in the inn to which it was joined.

For many centuries, prisoners were expected to contribute to their own upkeep in gaol, to the extent that courts could order the sale of inmate's goods and chattels to subsidise the cost of keeping them locked up. In April 1604, the Constable of Tuxford was ordered by the court to sell all the possessions of John Barker who was imprisoned in Nottingham Gaol 'for the relief and necessary maintenance of the same John, there expended'.

Under James I Act of 1609, it was mandatory that every county should provide a House of Correction to put the 'idle to work' and two years later Southwell's House of Correction opened its doors, later in 1806 it was enlarged, allowing it to house 150 prisoners. Nottingham's House of Correction, on St John's St, Sneinton, opened four years after Southwell's, but with only two rooms it was inadequate in its size.

The appointment as Governor of a House of Correction did not come without its problems, as Southwell's Governor found out on 12 April 1675, when it was ordered that if he 'does not show good cause for ye voluntary escape of Will Heiley at Newark Sessions yt hee bee [sic] bound to ye next Assizes at Nott'.

One of the problems with law and order was the lack of easy communication with law enforcement bodies and the distinct lack of willing constables who would take on this unpaid job. Petty Constables were required to take up their posts for one whole year to look after their parishes' needs when it became their turn. The position as a constable was taken in rotation by the male members of the community, and exemption would only be granted to the elderly, infirm or if a substitute could be found. Not everyone who took up the post did so with enthusiasm, as the constable of Fledborough proved in October 1615, when a warrant was issued against him after he failed to take a prisoner to the House of Correction because he 'negligently sent his wife with the prisoner, who escaped and fled

Arnold policemen. (Courtesy of Nottinghamshire County Council and www.picturethepast.org)

away'. The following year, the constable of North Leverton was fined 5s for pretending to be ill so he did not have to attend the sessions.

To alleviate the problem of keeping suspected criminals secure while his or her transfer to gaol could be arranged, many towns and villages had their own secure lock-up, where one or more cells would house the accused and the unruly. These lock-ups also helped the constable to maintain order because this is where he would put any drunkards to sober up overnight. The County Police Act of 1839 allowed county police forces to be formed and the use of the lock-up began to come to an end.

Even after a great deal of redevelopment, Nottingham's House of Correction was woefully overcrowded and conditions were inadequate, so a new prison was built at Bagthorpe which took all the prisoners from the House of Correction. It was in 1891 that the House of Correction finally closed its doors and was demolished.

Peatfield's Private Prison
The town of Bingham came close to disaster in 1710, when a local apothecary called Thomas Peatfield (aka Patesfield) took it upon himself to start three fires around the town, presumably in an attempt to cause as much damage as possible. Caught and arrested, he stood before the Assizes accused of arson – a very serious offence for which he had no excuse. Found guilty, but insane, he was sent to prison. However, two rooms were later built for him at the market place where he was kept until his death in 1739. Following Peatfield's death, his rooms were demolished and all traces have since gone.

The Hard Life of Hard Labour
As filthy and disease-ridden as they were, pre-Victorian prisons did at least allow communication between inmates, and any visitors that might venture inside – as well as the chance of bribing the gaolers to permit privileges adding to the hope of a more comfortable existence. The advent of the new style of gaols, and the systems employed, soon brought about a complete change in attitude towards the imprisoned and it rapidly became a regime of real hardship, not only physical but mental.

When the County House of Correction at Southwell was first built, the Regulations set down in 1619 stated that the Governor must '[…] sett them (the prisoners) on work by spinning and weaving of haircloth and sackcloth and by spinning of Jersey woollen or lynnen yarne […] whereby they may best earne their maintenance'. The Georgian perception of hard labour was strict; in 1779, the Penitentiary Act stated that: '[…] labour of the hardest and most servile kind in which drudgery is chiefly required and where the work is little liable to be spoiled by ignorance, neglect, or obstinacy […].' However, the Victorians decided that – with the crime rate rising at an alarming rate – prisons should become so unpleasant that it would act as a deterrent to anyone thinking of pursuing a life of crime, and the work that the prisoners were to be given would not only be unproductive but hard, boring and repetitive with no useful outcome. To ensure the convicts contemplated their terrible predicament, some gaols implemented the 'silent system', whereby prisoners were not able to speak to each other, nor identify each other because of the face masks and hoods they were made to wear —they were also given individual cells to further isolate them from each other. The Silent System was so effective in detaching the prisoners from each other, there were many instances of them going insane or mad, yet its implementation at Southwell was deemed a great success amongst the governor and wardens as discipline improved.

The courts issued the sentence of hard labour for many different types of crime, ranging from simple theft to vagrancy. In October 1883, twenty-six-year-old George Atkins of Nottingham, was given nine months' hard labour and one years' supervision for stealing a coach. Comparatively, earlier in the year, Mary Ann Sharpe was given two months' hard labour for stealing money from a till; there was no distinction in the severity of the crime when it came to administering hard labour. The prospect of what faced them in prison could not have been easy for the convicted – they were about to enter a world created to break their will by the sheer monotony of meaningless work.

Traditionally, everyone thinks of hard labour as men breaking rocks in a quarry all day with balls and a chain around their ankles to stop any escapes – sadly, the grim reality of it was far worse. Rock breaking could be included in the punishment regime, but, for the majority of convicts, the mind-destroying boredom of hard labour took place within the confines of the prison walls.

The hand crank consisted of a large box on top of a post on the side of which was a cranked handle that the prisoner had to turn relentlessly for hour after hour. On the front of the box was a counter that recalled the number of revolutions the handle had made. The frequently unreliable counter often registered fewer revolutions than had actually been made. Adults were required to make 14,400 turns of the handle, at a rate of 1,800 per hour, while juveniles did 12,000 in a day, at 1,500 revolutions per hour. If a prisoner was finding the task easy, the wardens could add weight to the handle by means of a screw mechanism – making the prisoner's work that much harder. It was this piece of machinery that led to the nickname of 'screw' for prison warders.

The shot drill involved bending over and picking up a cannon ball, walking a few steps and placing it back down before picking it up once more and replacing it in its original place. This was perhaps the most gruelling of punishments.

Oakum picking was possibly the most common of all hard labour duties in both regular prisons and prisons operating within the silent system. Though this task might appear less arduous than other types of hard labour, it could cause great pain, open sores and bleeding to the prisoner's hands. The oakum, old tarred rope from ships, was usually put in the convict's cell where he or she had to unpick the twisted rope into individual strands. After a short while their hands became covered in thick tar, making it difficult to work, and the chafing of the coarse fibres brought on sores and lesions that were made worse by the vigorous rubbing required to clean the sticky tar off their hands. The only comfort for the oakum picker was that the end product was put to good use as caulking for ships, stuffing for mattresses or it would be re-used in the manufacture of rope or string.

Although rudimentary treadmills had been in use for some years, Sir William Cubitt redesigned and reinvented the treadmill in 1817, after he noticed prisoners were idling their time away and thought that they should be reformed by 'teaching them habits of industry', and it was only a few short years before one was installed in a Nottinghamshire prison. Best described as being similar in design to a huge paddle-wheel, the treadmill was capable

Oakum picking.

Sir William Cubitt.

A Victorian prison treadmill.

of taking a large number of men standing side by side as they climbed the ever-rotating paddles for hours on end.

The House of Correction at Southwell was equipped with four treadmills – each one 5ft 4in in diameter with twenty-four steps around it, each one able to hold twelve prisoners, while four more prisoners waited their turn. In summer, every convict was expected to walk the treadmill for eight hours a day, and five hours of labour were expected every day in winter. Even the number of steps they took in a minute was regulated to thirty-six, which meant that, if a constant rate was kept up, each inmate could have done the equivalent of walking up a ladder in excess of 14,000ft. In 1824, the government was concerned that some prisoners were purposely injuring themselves to avoid working the treadmill and asked all prison surgeons to report any injuries caused by the work, so they could assess its usefulness.

On 31 December 1824, Dr B. Hutchinson wrote that, in the previous September, John Weightman of Southwell House of Correction was standing on the steps leading up to the treadmill when he stuck out his foot so far that the rotating board of the wheel caused him injury. The doctor concluded that because his injuries were slight, it had been an accident and no action was taken against Weightman.

When the Nottingham House of Correction had its treadmill installed in 1826, the convicts at least had the comfort of knowing their hard work was being put to a good use; their efforts were used to raise water up from a spring to provide supplies for the prison and a public tap that was used outside. In comparison to Southwell's treadmill, Nottingham's was the more arduous – by the end of a shift treading the wheel each prisoner would have climbed 15,120ft at an almost vertical angle.

Should any prisoner be brave enough to refuse to take their turn on the wheel, their milk allowance was forfeited and so were any earnings they would have accrued.

Hard labour came to end in English prisons in 1898, with the Prison Reform Act, which changed the attitude on imprisonment from that of deterrent and subjugation through repetitive activity, to one of reforming.

The Ones that Got Away

Escape is something that most convicts frequently thought of and that many tried. A lot of those that made a bid for freedom failed to get very far, but, once in a while, luck was on the side of the prisoner and a life in gaol was left far behind. It was then up to the gaoler or escort to try to explain away the unfortunate incident that had befallen them. Occasionally the humiliation of allowing an escape was made very public as William Read, the Constable of Bulwell Parish, found to his embarrassment when he was forced to place the following advertisement in *Creswell's Nottingham and Newark Journal* in 1773:

PARDON

I, William Read, Constable of the Parish of Bullwell in the County of Nottingham, having about a Month ago, by Virtue of a Warrant under the Hand and Seal of Thomas Charlton Esq.; one of his Majesty's Justices of the Peace for the County of Nottingham, apprehended and taken up Joseph Blackuock, Joseph Carnell, Matthias Carnell, William Morris, John Wildgoose, James Brecknock, and Samuel Dawes, for a Misdemeanour, the two latter of whom I permitted to escape, for which Offence I deservedly ought to have been severely punished. But in Consideration of my Submission, and due Acknowledgement of the Offence, the said Tho [*sic*] Charlton Esq; hath stayed all further Proceedings against me. Now I do hereby publickly [*sic*] confess my Misconduct, and ask Pardon for the same, and do most sincerely promise that I will be particularly attentive for the future, in the Discharge of my official Duty, and render to the Publick [*sic*] every Recompense in my Power, by a dutiful and proper Behaviour.

As Witness my Hand, this 11th Day of July, 1773, William Read.

Witness, Samuel Turner:

Who Wants the Job Anyway?

Whatever his faults, William Read did appear to take his responsibilities seriously enough to answer for his failings when he allowed his prisoners to escape, but not every constable felt that way. Edward Caley of Rolleston was in the unenviable position of constable when he was ordered to appear before the courts in April 1605, for setting one of his prisoners free. He defended himself by claiming he was given the order to allow the prisoner to go by 'Mr Sutton's man' – an excuse that the judge was unwilling to believe, so he instructed Caley to bring proof of his claim to the next sessions.

Caley's next visit to the Sessions in July brought him more misery when his outburst of 'I will fynde [*sic*] another knave to execute my busynesse [*sic*] of constable' left him with a fine of 10s. Sadly, there is no record to say whether Caley was able to prove his innocence over the release of his prisoner.

A Policeman's Lot is Not a Happy One

With the advent of a professional police force in the nineteenth century, it soon became apparent that discipline was essential to uphold the standards of the force, and to earn the respect of the people who they were there to protect. Sometimes, though, those standards slipped a little leading to disciplinary action being taken against the lax policeman.

On Christmas day 1893, Constable Thomas Bingham of the City of Nottingham Police was found drunk, behaving in an insubordinate manner and wearing his uniform when off duty. For his over indulgence, he was fined one weeks' pay, but less than two years later in August 1895, he received a caution for selling a dog without permission that he had found wandering around. Undaunted by his experience, he continued in the force but was once more in trouble in February 1897, when he was discovered intoxicated while on parade. For this third offence, he was fined 15s. Despite his lack of self- discipline, PC Bingham settled down to a successful career and retired in 1921 as an Inspector.

Fortunately, PC Ford was allowed to apologise for his actions when accused of gossiping with a civilian while on duty and failing to attend a chimney fire, but PC Ives had to do a lot more explaining when he was caught in a rather embarrassing situation. For discreditable conduct and neglect of duty, Ives was given a reduction in pay for a whole year after he was observed in a women's lodging house for three-quarters of an hour and for entering the bedroom of a prostitute. He was also charged with not working his beat for the time in which he was in the house.

Not everyone is suited to a career of law enforcement and all that it entails, as PC Denyer was to show when he was transferred for showing a distinct lack of enthusiasm for his profession. The hapless constable had put in less effort than was required to arrest a prisoner who had been creating a breach of the peace and had assaulted a fellow office – it was Denyer's reluctance to put any energy into his work that led to him facing disciplinary action.

Military Justice

In July 1805, an army deserter escaped from his guards near Harlow Wood, when under escort while on his way to face trial in Mansfield. As the deserter ran into the undergrowth in a bid for freedom the Corporal in charge of the escort shouted out for him to stop and return. Ignoring the warning, the deserter carried on in his bid for freedom until the Corporal fired his musket and shot him dead.

Transportation and Exile

Until the advent of large prisons and the infrastructure capable of housing a great number of inmates, the problem of what to do with convicted criminals remained a problem. It was with the discovery of new lands and colonies far across the sea that the idea of transportation was born. The Conventicles Act of 1664 was one of the first pieces of legislation that imposed transportation on convicts. Other than in a church of the Church of England, it was illegal for more than five people (except a family in its home) to gather together for religious purposes. First offenders were fined £5 or three months in prison, second offenders faced a £10 fine or six months in prison, while third time offenders were fined £100 or transported for seven years.

The convict hulk Success *in Hobart.*
(Courtesy of National Library of Australia)

Transported secondary convicts' uniform.
(National Library of Australia)

The idea of transportation usually evokes thoughts of convicts being exiled to Australia to live in a wild and untamed country – never to return to their homeland. In some cases this was true, but, for a great number of convicts, transportation was only a temporary term of imprisonment that, once completed, gave them the option of staying in Australia or returning home. Until the American War of Independence, any man or woman sentenced to be transported could expect, in the main, to be sent to the West Indies or America; it was not until Great Britain lost control of its colony in the New World that the government's attention turned to Australia. The only transported convicts who could not return to England under pain of death, were those sentenced to transportation for life, or convicts who escaped and made their own way home. If discovered, the escaped convict could expect a date with the hangman – as absconder Richard Wheatley found out on 30 March 1774.

Convicted in 1768 of breaking into Mr Morton's pie shop in Nottingham, Wheatley was sentenced to transportation to Maryland in America, where he was, in turn, sold as a slave to work on a ship. Enthusiastic and willing to learn, he soon became skilled as a sailor until he was press-ganged by the Royal Navy to serve in Admiral Rodney's fleet, which, at that time, was sailing out of the West Indies. After serving his time onboard one of Rodney's warships, he was transferred to a merchant ship which returned him to England in 1772 – four years after his departure. Making his way northwards, Wheatley found gainful employment in Loughborough, but his experiences over the previous four years had failed to teach him a lesson and he soon went back into his old ways of burglary. Following a robbery on a bleach yard he was arrested, but his previous conviction was soon discovered, and, despite all he had gone through, he was hanged for returning to England before the term of his transportation had been completed.

Transportation to the colonies was given for all manner of crimes, whether it was a minor infringement or something more serious. April 1808 saw William Barr found guilty of larceny at the Assizes, so he was transported to Australia for seven years. In 1814, George Sheppard also received seven years in Australia for 'larceny from the person', while, two years earlier, George Spray was given fourteen years for 'feloniously breaking stocking frames'. Any family or dependants left behind would have to fend for themselves or hope they could impose on the parish.

Once a conviction had been passed, the prisoners were first taken to hulk ships – dismasted merchant ships that were converted into floating prisons – to await a convict ship that would take them to their final destination. With the hulks riding at anchor mainly on the Thames and Portsmouth, conditions onboard were atrocious with the threat of disease a constant worry. Any prisoner taken ill was transferred to the hospital ship nearby, another floating death trap where it was safer not to be admitted.

On 28 June 1842, Thomas Bird had been sentenced at the Nottingham Assizes to ten years' imprisonment but it was not until 8 April 1844, almost two years later that he was received onto the prison hulk *Fortitude*. Conditions on the Fortitude could not have agreed with Bird, for, on 22 February 1846, his health had deteriorated so much so he was put on the hospital ship *Unite*. At 3.09 a.m. on 4 April 1846, he died.

Bird was one of many who paid with his life for the terrible conditions that had to be endured on the hulks and in the gaols of the nineteenth century, and age was no respecter to someone's well being either. Sixty-four-year-old Joseph Barks had been given a ten-year gaol term at his trial in Newark in October 1843, which led to him being transferred to Millbank prison near London on 23 December 1843. By 1 November 1845, his condition had become so serious he was moved to the *Unite*, moored nearby. Barks lingered on in poor health until he finally died at 12.15 a.m. on 29 April 1846, far away from his family and probably unattended.

—Seven—

CHURCHLY GOINGS-ON

Church Courts

The influence of the Church, and the power that it held within courts, led many God-fearing citizens to stay on the side of caution instead of stepping out of line, in case it meant some humiliating form of punishment, but not everyone was so fearful of the penalty that might have been imposed should they be caught, and some carried on their lives with gay abandon. The lives of our ancestors were ruled and dominated by the Church Courts and its influence continued at least, in part, until the middle of the nineteenth century. In today's legal system where there are a number different levels of court (Magistrate's Court, County Court etc), the Church Courts also had a similar form of hierarchy.

Dealing mainly with matters of a moral nature and cases of impropriety these courts gained the nickname of the 'Bawdy Courts'. In October 1581, Thomas Campson of Bridgford was taken before the court and accused of 'misusing his wyfe [sic]' when he failed to fulfil his sexual duties of marriage. Campson denied the accusation and pleaded not guilty. Unfortunately for him, his wife's side of the story was believed, and he was ordered to go home and do his duty or face the full force of the law. Neither Thomas Campson nor his wife returned to court, so we must assume he managed to gain the will and strength to satisfy his wife.

John Tynker of Blythe had even more incentive to abide by the courts' ruling when he too was accused of not giving his all to his wife. Admitting that he lived apart from his spouse, he was ordered to move back in and live 'conjugally' with her and 'to fetche her againe [sic]'. If he failed in his wife's satisfaction, he was to be fined £10. Just like Thomas Campson, John Tynker had no need to return to court, so it looks like he too managed to summon some inner strength.

There seems to have been some strange kind of bias towards extra marital activities that brought about some unusual outcomes. At a court hearing in January 1577, Edmund Birkett must have thought all his prayers had been answered when he found himself in bed with two women one night. Once his indiscretion had been discovered, he was hauled before the court where he admitted all three of them had been 'making meary [sic] together'. One of the women was his own wife while the other was his neighbour's wife. When Burkett's wife disclosed it had been her idea the case was dismissed.

Benefit of Clergy

First introduced in the twelfth century to avoid having to face criminal prosecution in secular courts, clerics would claim benefit of clergy to ensure they faced prosecution in front of an ecclesiastical court. Ecclesiastical courts were more lenient than their secular counterparts, and the accused cleric took advantage of this to avoid the death penalty – which would have been imposed if he or she had not chosen to take the benefit. Many criminals disguised themselves as a cleric to take advantage of the ruling, but, due to the difficulty in actually deciding who of the accused was within the Church and who was not, the accused was required to read a passage from the Bible to prove their literacy and education. Judges traditionally chose a verse from the 51st Psalm which gave rise to it being called the 'Neck Verse' because of the number of necks that were saved from the hangman's noose when it was successfully read aloud.

During a heavy drinking session in 1532, Prior Richard Sherwood of the Carmelite Friary in Nottingham killed Friar William Bacon. Luckily for Sherwood, the King gave him a pardon, but, even if he had been made to stand trial, he would have claimed benefit of clergy and, in all probability, escaped severe punishment.

With the widespread abuse of benefit of clergy, its implementation fell into disrepute, and it gradually became used less and less until its abolition in 1827.

Penance

Many of the men and women who were brought before the courts, and found guilty as charged, were ordered to do penance as punishment. The whole principal of penance was to publicly humiliate the guilty person in a ritualistic ceremony in order to show how remorseful and penitent they were. Each part of the ceremony was calculated to bring upon the head of the penitent more and more disgrace.

The story of Margery Billadge from Car Colston, is typical of the ritual that had to be performed by the penitent, when she was ordered to attend church for morning prayers on 23 May 1591 – dressed only in a white sheet. She was to carry a white rod, be bareheaded, barefooted and barelegged and while the congregation listened to the service she was to kneel in full view of them. Once the service was over, Billadge was made to stand on some form of furniture so that she could be seen by everyone and recite a passage, prepared on her behalf, beseeching forgiveness for having sex with William Sommer when out of wedlock. To add to her humiliation, she had to go through the whole thing again the following week at Screveton and then once more a week later back at Car Colston.

William Collington of Gamston underwent his penance for threatening William Oliver with a dagger while in the churchyard, but perhaps one of the contenders for most penances goes to Thomas Lee of Bilsthorpe, who pleaded guilty to having had a sexual relationship and having lived with his wife's sister. In September 1583, just eight years before Margery Billadge's penance, Lee was ordered to do penance in Nottingham market place on Saturday, Newark market place on Wednesday, Mansfield market place on Thursday and Retford market place on the following Saturday. If this was not enough, he was instructed to do another four penances at his own parish church on four Sundays, and to top it all off one each at 'Eykringe and Winckbourne'. It is easy to imagine Lee's reaction to his sentence, especially if he was aware of the leniency that Edmund Birkett had been dealt with in his case.

Excommunication

One way of punishing a member of the congregation who stepped out of line was to excommunicate them. During court proceedings it was invariably imposed on the accused who failed to turn up for the hearing, or who failed to carry out their punishment if pronounced guilty. Its implementation for the deeply religious had a profound effect, as it barred them from the congregation and the religious community to which they belonged. Not everyone was frightened of the prospect of never going to church again, though. Richard Flinton of Newark showed his disrespect for the Church and its laws when, in September 1635, he beat up Gilbert Hinton with a cudgel. His situation was made all the worse since he attacked Hinton inside the church as the service was going on. When Flinton failed to turn up for his trial, he was excommunicated never returning to have the excommunication lifted.

Sometimes the threat of being excommunicated had the desired effect and the guilty party would duly turn up and take their punishment. January 1754 saw Anne Jilman of Lenton brought before the Archdeaconry court, charged with having given birth to an illegitimate child. Unable to hide the obvious, she was sentenced to do penance, something that she was reluctant to do. When Jilman failed to turn up and perform her penance the court duly excommunicated her. The severity of her future within the Church finally hit home and on 29 July – just two weeks after her excommunication was announced – she appeared in church to do her penance. Alas for Jilman, this was not the end of the matter; due to her failure to follow the court's instructions, she was ordered to pay the court's costs of 11s. It was not until 11 August, eight months after her original trial, that Anne Jilman's troubled times were over.

Compergators

A clever way of avoiding punishment when accused of a crime, was by the use of compergators. A compergator was a character witness that was produced by the accused in their defence against any supposed offence. The person standing trial would strongly deny any charges, and, to show their good character, a specified number of compergators, as ordered by the judge, would be brought into court and under oath they would testify to the good standing and behaviour of the accused.

November 1584 saw James Hartley of North Collingham, charged with drunkenness, with being a common drunkard, for swearing and for being a 'sower of discord'. For pleading not guilty he was ordered to prove his innocence by providing six compergators for each offence. Fortunately, Hartley had enough friends to call upon who swore to his good character.

Not everyone who stood before the judge and protested their innocence was able to satisfy the requirements needed to avoid punishment though. In February 1619, John Ludlam of Trowell was taken to court for sending Richard Nixston to see a wizard. Richard Nixston was in turn prosecuted for taking his friends advice and visiting the supposed man of magic. When neither man could produce any compurgators, both of them were ordered to do penance.

Don't Enjoy the Sabbath

Not all were devout enough to studiously attend church each and every Sunday, and the temptation to indulge in a bit of merrymaking was too much to resist for many people. The court records are full of cases where too much enjoyment has been punished. In June 1587, John Bourne of Warsop was prosecuted for playing his pipes during service time and for his efforts he was made to donate 6d to the poor box.

Edward Fitzwilliams went one step further and played cards in his local alehouse when he should have been at church. When he failed to attend court he was excommunicated.

Six men from Bradmore were charged in November 1618, for Morris dancing on the Sabbath, and, although their sentence and the sentence of their pipers is not known, the fate of Richard Mee of Wollaton is there for all to see. Just days before the men from Bradmore stood before the judge, Mee had pleaded guilty to being in the company of Morris dancers. After he was ordered to do penance and to pay the court costs, Mee decided that he had better things to do and refused to obey the ruling. The judge promptly had him excommunicated.

Occasionally, the lure of the outdoors would become too strong for some of the congregation and it was not a rare occurrence for the judge to have before him a self-styled sportsman. July 12 1577 saw William Clayton, John Studysburye, Richard Collingham and Alan Hemstocke of Edwinstowe presented for playing bowls when they should have been at the evening service the previous Whit Sunday. They all pleaded guilty and were ordered to pay 12d each into the poor box.

A reminder about having too much fun.

John Smith from Blythe faired a little better in 1617 when he was accused of playing bowls and fishing on the Sabbath. Smith managed to escape with a warning.

The Rector is a Thief

The sixteenth and seventeenth centuries were possibly the most frustrating for the Church authorities. The continuing stream of moral outrages that were brought before the bench must have been a constant source of frustration, but once in a while a more serious matter would arise. At the court sessions on 29 October 1583, the unnamed Rector of South Collingham, stood before his accusers charged with stealing the lead from the chancel roof. Unable to deny the charge he pleaded guilty and was commanded to make a large donation of 30s to the poor box within one month and to have the lead replaced on the chancel roof. If he failed to carry out the order, he was to suffer the 'pain of the law'.

Not in Church Please

Attending church was supposed to be a spiritually uplifting exercise that led to renewed friendships and harmony amongst the worshippers, whilst the vicar traditionally gave a fire and brimstone sermon warning against sin and temptation. Unfortunately, at times, someone seems to have forgotten to tell the congregation how things were supposed to work.

William Frithe, Robert Mount, Robert Newbolde, William Wyndell and Richard Wyggen, all from Nottingham, must have forgotten they were in church when they started arguing. Hauled before the judge in June 1572, they all pleaded guilty and were told to reconcile themselves in front of the curate and the church wardens after first taking Holy Communion.

At the opposite end of the extreme, it was also against the rules to have fun in church as William Stockley of Clifton found out in July 1618. Stockley was dismissed with a warning after he laughed aloud in the church.

Even the best of clergymen can sometimes produce a sermon that can only be described as boring and tedious, so perhaps that is why William Lee, Anthony Wharton, Robert Gybsone and Jeneta Greena all fell asleep during the service. The upset clergy had them prosecuted in court, where a slightly sympathetic judge advised them to make known their faults in church the following Sunday.

For anyone to quarrel during a church service must take quite a bit of provocation, so what could have sparked off Richard Flinton's reaction to Gilbert Hinton? On 11 September 1635, Flinton of Newark failed to turn up at court to defend himself on the charge of beating Hinton with a cudgel during a sermon. His failure to present himself at court led to his excommunication.

Punishing the Vicar

The position of trust bestowed on a vicar has been taken for granted for many years, but that situation has been abused by more than one incumbent down the years. Only Lords and high-ranking nobles were entitled to hunt for deer during the middle ages and it was a risky venture to go poaching for venison –death or mutilation were often meted out to the perpetrator. In 1334, John de Roystan, the vicar of Edwinstowe, was found guilty of 'venison trespasses'; unfortunately, there is no record of his fate.

Some years later the vicar of Rolleston, John Butterfield, was prohibited from entering the church. He had been charged with being stubbornly and wilfully disobedient to authority, so, when his trial came on 20 August 1521, it should have come as no surprise that he failed to turn up.

Bell Ringing Rancour

The sound of church bells ringing away brings with it the image of the faithful making their way to Sunday service, of christenings, funerals and a whole host of other church events. Before the advent of the accurate, easily affordable timepiece, the sound of the bells was the signal for the devoted to make their way to church. In May 1588, William Bolton of Elkesley made such a racket when ringing the bells he was presented at court on a charge of 'ringing the belles unorderly [sic] to the disturbance of the parish'. To top it off, he was also found guilty of playing football in the churchyard. The parishioners of Elkesley came off best after Bolton was made to put 10s into the poor box.

Burial Woes

An executor of a will is often chosen for their honesty and their talent in being able to cope with a potentially distressing situation. It has always been the duty of an executor to follow through with the wishes of the deceased's will, regardless of the executors own wishes. June 1670 saw Richard Greaves of South Collingham given the task of fulfilling the duties of executor when Henry Booth, his wife Elizabeth Booth and their son all died within a short time of each other. After having successfully got his friends buried in the parish church, he then refused to pay the three nobles (equivalent to £1) for their burials. Failing to turn up at his trial, he was excommunicated, probably deciding it was more profitable to stay away and keep the money rather than turn up and be fined.

In order to protect the woollen trade, Charles II introduced the Burials in Woollen Acts of 1667 and 1668, which instructed that all bodies (except those who had died from the plague) must be buried in a sheep wool shroud. Failure to comply would lead to a fine of £5 against the deceased's estate and anyone involved in the burial. Robert Brough became the first to be 'wound in fflannell [sic] at Hucknall' when he was buried on 20 August 1678. The Woollen Acts were repealed in 1814, although by that time it had been generally ignored for over forty years.

Divine Intervention?

The use of bad or foul language inside a church, or churchyard, has frequently brought down the wrath of the authorities on the head of the perpetrator. Take the case of Thomas Poole and Alexander Dyckinson of Tollerton who, in September 1580, were found fighting and quarrelling in the churchyard. During the argument, Dyckinson gave Poole a hefty punch to the nose causing a nosebleed. This riotous affair brought down the customary excommunication on both their heads. Times had not changed when, in June 1621, John Gervis of Broughton Sulney was arraigned for swearing in the chancel. His admission of guilt brought with it the retribution of penance.

Was divine intervention responsible for Godfrey Lache's escape from castigation after a rather unfortunate outburst? Lache incurred the anger of his church in Worksop when, in

1637, he refused to 'bowe [*sic*] the knee at the name of Jesus at the tyme [*sic*] of the reading of the Gospell [*sic*] or at any other part of the service'. Admonished by the incumbent at the time he replied that he could 'sitt [*sic*] on my arse and doe [*sic*] it'. The case against Lache was dismissed. Divine intervention?

A Visitation of God

Coroner's inquests can sometimes be traumatic and perplexing – especially when the cause of death is hard to establish. Take, for instance, the sad tale of Elizabeth Purday, who attended church with her daughter at the Methodist Church at Hill Top, Newthorpe in April 1837. While Purday sat in the main body of the church, her daughter took a seat in the gallery overlooking. It was towards the end of the sermon, during the evening service, that Purday's daughter became overcome and fainted, causing a little commotion, so some kindly people carried her down into the main body of the church where her mother was. A member of the congregation noticed Elizabeth Purday's head fall backwards as she sat in her seat and a quick examination showed that she was dead. An inquest delivered a verdict of natural death 'by the sudden visitation of God'.

December 1865 saw a similar verdict given when, eighty-four-year-old Samuel Reed, died inside Gedling Church. Reed took his place in his pew and was then heard by the Parish Clerk to fall to the ground. When the Clerk went to check on Reed, he found that he had expired on the spot.

A Victorian funeral.

George Fox

Apprenticed to a shoemaker in Nottingham around 1635, the young George Fox soon began to question his own religious beliefs, and whether he could find all he spiritually needed within the church as it stood. Taking up the wandering life of an itinerant shoemaker, he began to travel in the hope of finding answers to his many questions. Unable to gain satisfaction from the clergy that he came upon and quizzed, he gradually became more convinced they could never give him the answers he craved for. At some point in 1647, he had the revelation that he must spread the word that everything and everyone in authority was corrupt, there was to be no distinction between the Church and state — as both were equally guilty. Fox's loud and impassioned speeches about the failings of the Church and state soon gained him a small but loyal following who called themselves *The Friends of Truth*, later to be known as the Quakers.

George Fox.

Fox's reputation for plain speaking went ahead of him, and, as he toured around the countryside, he received a mixed reception, sometimes he was welcomed but more often the crowd was hostile. On one visit to Mansfield Woodhouse in 1649, he attempted to have his say on the Church, whereupon he was given a sound beating, put in the stocks and finally stoned until he left the village. In the same year, he was making his way through Nottingham when he came upon St Mary's Church as a service was taking place. Making the decision to enter the church and to listen to the service, he was soon incensed enough to stand up and rebuke the preacher pointing out his mistakes. At that time it was a requirement to wait until the end of the service to voice an opinion, otherwise it was an arrestable offence to interrupt. Fox was duly arrested, tried and sent to prison where he described the gaol as 'a nasty stinking place'. Luckily for Fox, his time in the gaol was short-lived, simply because he managed to convert Sheriff Reckless and his wife to his way of thinking. After a stay in Reckless' house, Fox moved on to spread his word and in the process to receive more imprisonment, more beatings and more punishment. Ironically, Reckless took up Fox's mantle in Nottingham and often preached his mentors teachings in the market place.

Sanctuary

Before 1624, anyone accused of committing a crime could escape their persecutors by claiming the right of sanctuary within a church. Whether the alleged criminal was guilty or not did not matter to the Church, as they acted as intermediaries between the accused and the accusers in an effort to resolve the situation. Many minor crimes, such as receiving stolen goods or making late payments, allowed the fleeing felon to seek sanctuary in any church but, for more serious crimes like murder, horse stealing and debt the only true hope of reprieve was to travel as far as Beverley in Yorkshire, where the rights of sanctuary

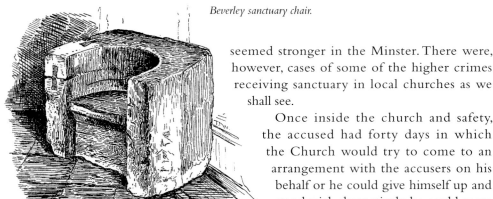

Beverley sanctuary chair.

seemed stronger in the Minster. There were, however, cases of some of the higher crimes receiving sanctuary in local churches as we shall see.

Once inside the church and safety, the accused had forty days in which the Church would try to come to an arrangement with the accusers on his behalf or he could give himself up and stand trial, alternatively he could agree to exile. The penalty for claiming the protection of the church was the loss of all goods and possessions to the Crown. In Beverley Minster, the maximum time for sanctuary was thirty days but, regardless of who provided protection to the fugitive, once exile had been chosen he would be given a white wooden cross to hold and then taken by the constable and placed in the custody of the next constable on the route. This process was carried out many times until the person facing exile reached the nearest seaport and was placed on the first available ship. It was, theoretically, possible to claim sanctuary three times, however, on the third time of claiming it the runaway had to commit his life to the service of the church.

John de Colston of Nottingham managed to successfully escape from the gaol in town after he was accused of murdering the wife of Henry de Pek in 1329. Colston was able to make his way to Beverley and claim sanctuary, while in 1393, Henry de Whitby (or Whalley) took refuge in the Carmelite Friary in Nottingham after murdering his wife. In that same year, John Leveret managed to escape from custody in Nottingham and he too claimed sanctuary in the Friary.

One shrewd killer from Mansfield, John Strynger, took refuge within the confines of Norwell church in 1369, and claimed the right of sanctuary. Strynger's wish for a safe haven was granted on condition he left the country within seven days by using the port of Dover.

As late as 1535, Beverley was still being used by Nottinghamshire men as a means to escape prosecution when Robert Warren of Nottingham fled there to avoid his debts.

Not everyone who claimed sanctuary fulfilled the requirements of leaving the realm by the quickest route, and for those who took the chance to earn a quick living on their way to the port the consequences could be catastrophic. Two outlaws who took sanctuary in Newark church in 1290, were given a specified route to the nearest port by which they should leave the country. Regrettably, the two outlaws decided to commit one more robbery while they travelled on their way. After a chase the two were captured and beheaded.

The right of sanctuary gradually lost its powers through the reigns of various monarchs until James I finally did away with it for criminal cases.

Terrible Tithes

The control of the Church over everyday life in England brought with it a great deal of resentment amongst the peasant farmers. Not only was the peasant expected to work on church lands for free they were, in addition to this, expected to give one tenth of their income to the local clergy – either in money or by supplying one tenth of all their crops. This reluctance to part with hard earned cash or food led to many legal cases where the vicar took the non payer to court. Stephen Coe, the rector of Ordsall, had no reluctance in prosecuting none payers when on 21 July 1599, he took Michael Younge and John Brome of Babworth, to court for withholding tithes. Two months later on 22 September, Brome failed to appear in court and was excommunicated, whereas Younge paid up.

The persistent Coe was once more in action in 1605, when he brought Nicholas Younge to task for non payment of his tithes. Younge took the decision to avoid court and he too was excommunicated.

Even during the times of Oliver Cromwell and the Commonwealth the clergy freely took actions against reluctant tithe payers when, in April 1658, John Kirk, vicar of Eaton, took to court Robert Murfin who had withheld payments for several years. Murfin was ordered to pay the arrears of £1 6s 10d.

The reintroduction of the monarchy in 1660 brought no relief to the peasant farmers and tithes still had to be paid – and still payments were not made, sometimes for years. John Camme of Maplebeck felt the fury of the courts when, in April 1697, the Curate of Maplebeck, Robert Parker, followed through with his threat of prosecution. Camme had not paid his dues to the church for four years and finding him guilty the judge ordered he pay the full amount of £1 2s 6d.

—Eight—

RIGHT ROYAL TROUBLES

Monarchical positions in days-gone-by required strength, poise, intelligence, cunning, guile, and a smattering of luck. Not all of those that gained the crown came with these assets and fewer still were able to put these abilities to use in peaceful or constructive ways, finding it easier, and possibly necessary, to use harsh and often violent means to keep control. Pity, then, the monarch that used capital and corporal punishment, (as well as some other forms of retribution) too freely, would find that, in some cases, it would come back to haunt them. For centuries, Nottinghamshire had seen the rise and demise of many of the ruling elite, with their personal ambitions and insecurities leading to the downfall of many of their innocent (and not-so-innocent) subjects.

If legend is correct, the first Royal that is known to have fallen foul of Nottinghamshire's turbulent past is King Edwin of Northumberland. In October 633, he was killed by the forces of Penda of Mercia and Cadwalla of Gwynedd at the battle of Hatfield (Cuckney). His followers quickly buried his body in a woodland clearing nearby so that his enemies could not take it as a trophy. Their intentions were to return at a later date and retrieve his corpse for burial elsewhere. The place close to where his body was interred now carries the name Edwinstowe (*Edwin's resting place*). In 1951, the remains of over 200 young men were discovered buried together underneath the church at Cuckney – it looks like a large number of Edwin's soldiers shared their master's fate and died with him.

Many a sovereign has come to grief in Nottinghamshire, but so have many of their subjects and to be at the wrong end of an irate king or queen's justice was to ensure a very rough kind of injustice. Pity then the man or woman that had to bear the personal wrath of a ruler that felt slighted by their actions and pity more those that were innocent.

'Good' King John

When King Richard died in 1199 and his younger brother John took over the throne, the country as a whole let out a collective groan and wondered what they were in for. John already had the reputation for cruelty and greed and now he was in charge of the whole show. Regarded by many to be a poor and inferior replacement for his brother, he was now able to make decisions and take actions that infuriated vast swathes of his people.

In 1191, while Richard had been on the crusades, his brother had tried to seize power by taking control of a number of castles, including Nottingham, and when news came the

King John by Matthew Paris.

following year that Richard had been captured, it looked like all John's wishes had come true. Sadly for John, Richard managed to return to England in early 1194 and immediately set about retaking Nottingham Castle. Some of those captured after the surrender were held for ransom, others were fined, while some had to find pledges of 100 marks. All in all they got off quite lightly but once Richard had finally died John was able to put into practice his own forms of justice.

During his reign, King John had many troubles with the Welsh continually rising up in rebellion, so, in order to keep the Welsh Princes subjugated, he had the sons of the leading Welsh Chieftains taken prisoner and kept as hostages in Nottingham Castle. It was, without doubt, that John's darkest hour came in 1212, when, after being given the news of yet another revolt in Wales, he held a meeting just outside Clipstone and, deciding on a course of action, he rode in anger to Nottingham intent on taking retribution for the Welsh disloyalty. Entering the castle, he ordered all twenty-eight boys, ranging in age from twelve to fourteen, to be executed. The petrified boys were dragged to the castle walls to hang, pleading for mercy all the while. As cruel and inhumane as this act was, Matthew Paris tells the tale of Geoffrey – a clerk of the Exchequer who was cast in Nottingham castle's dungeon – whereupon 'He closed him in leade [*sic*], and so, by depryvinge [*sic*] him of al ayre [*sic*] bereft him of his life withal'. There was no real evidence that Geoffrey had committed any crime.

It was with some relief and joy to many of his subjects that 'Good King John' finally got his comeuppance at Newark. In September 1216, John was vigorously attempting to quell yet another rebellion amongst his Barons when he contracted dysentery. Crossing the Wash, John is said to have lost his Crown Jewels and treasures and as his health deteriorated he and his supporters made their way to Newark where, on October 18, he died. Legend has it that, as he lay inside the castle, he drew his last breath in agony as a gale raged outside. Many reasons were rumoured to be the cause of his passing; eating a 'surfeit of peaches', eating poisoned or bad plums, or drinking poisoned ale, and yet the most plausible cause of his death was a terrible and acute case of dysentry.

Henry VII and the Last Battle

The Wars of the Roses lasted for over thirty years and for noblemen making the choice to back one side or the other could ultimately lead to receiving glory and riches or disgrace and a brutal death. We are told the culmination of this decades long conflict happened on 22 August 1485, when Henry Tudor led his Lancastrian forces in, successfully defeating Richard III's Yorkist army at the Battle of Bosworth. The hopes of a Yorkist victory were

The battlefield of East Stoke, looking down from the rebel high ground.

dashed when Richard was killed while bravely trying to attack and kill his opponent Henry Tudor. With his enemy dead, Henry grabbed the throne of England and proclaimed himself King Henry VII – king of a still divided country.

By early 1487, however, after numerous problems it was plain to see that war was again a possibility when a general restlessness swept over the country and reports began that an invasion fleet was being assembled on the continent.

When it came, the invading force of Yorkist supporters was led by the ambitious John De La Pole, Earl of Lincoln, whose main driving force was his desire to claim power for himself or his family. His forces landed near Furness in Lancashire on 4 June, and, as the rebels began their forced march southwards, King Henry began to gather his forces and to plan his next move.

At the head of Lincoln's forces was the supposed Earl of Warwick, a young boy who was seen by true Yorkists as the rightful king and someone who could lead the country into a new era. Unbeknown to most of those around though, was that Warwick was an impostor. This young boy of about ten has been given the name Lambert Simnel by history, yet his real name remains a mystery. This was all a very clever ploy by Lincoln and others to usurp Henry with a pretender.

On 14 June, whilst camped outside Nottingham, a rumour went through Henry's army claiming that he had abandoned them and left them to their fate. When he returned to camp and was told of the malicious gossip he knew he had to act fast and hard so, to quell any unrest, he had the rumour mongers and any spies that could be found hanged on an ash tree at the end of Nottingham Bridge.

By nine o'clock in the morning on 16 June, Lincoln's army had taken up their positions at the top of a rise at Stoke just outside Newark, while Henry's leading forces took up position slightly to the east ready for the onslaught that would surely come. The battle began in earnest with a downhill charge by the rebels intending to sweep away all resistance before them, but, vastly outnumbered, it was only a matter of time before they began to waver and within three hours it was all over. Henry never actually took part in the fighting, instead favouring to watch from a safe distance from either the top of a church tower or, maybe, even from the top of a windmill. When he did at last venture onto the battle field, it was all over and the utter carnage he saw must have shaken him because he never dismounted from his horse – instead, he turned and rode off. Somewhere between 4,000 and 7,000 of Lincoln's forces died that day, while only a few hundred of Henry's perished.

King Henry went to Newark and bestowed honours on his allies while the German mercenaries were sent home – after all, Henry might need them one day himself – any English or Irish were hanged. Lambert Simnel, the alleged Earl of Warwick, was at first imprisoned in Newark and then the Tower of London. His punishment was to be given employment in the Kings kitchens, possibly at first as a turnspit, until he finally rose to be the king's falconer. Up to twenty-eight of the minor nobles that supported the uprising lost all their estates to the Crown, while more high ranking men were either pardoned or bought safety. The main protagonists in the Yorkist camp were killed in the battle, but mystery surrounded the disappearance of Viscount Lovell. At the time it was suggested he had drowned while trying to cross the River Trent in a vain attempt at escape. However, by a strange twist of events, a body was found walled up in Minster Lovell Castle during works undertaken in the eighteenth century. When discovered, the body was said to be sat at a table with a dog at its feet.

The doorway of East Stoke Church, where it is said the rebel soldiers sharpened their swords before the battle.

The memorial to the dead of the Battle of East Stoke.

The Dissolution of the Monasteries

Henry VIII is perhaps best known for his six wives and how he treated four of them as if they were disposable objects. As the old rhyme goes: 'Divorced, beheaded, died, divorced, beheaded, survived.' Add to this Henry's decision to break the English Church away from Rome, and the recipe for centuries of religious turmoil was set. The catalyst for the severing of ties with Rome was the Pope's refusal to allow Henry a divorce from his first wife, the Catholic Catherine of Aragon, in order to allow him to marry the Protestant Anne Boleyn.

The break with Rome came in 1534, when the Act of Supremacy was passed, making Henry the Supreme Head of the Church of England. One of the main forces behind this change was Anne Boleyn herself, at the time Henry's lover, but she also had influential and powerful allies to help her in the guise of Thomas Cromwell and Thomas Cranmer. Born at Aslockton, near Nottingham, into a minor gentry family, Cranmer had started off with quite a poor education but had worked hard to make his way to the top. His academic prowess was without question and he proved himself to be an able ally to Henry as he sought to end his marriage from Catherine. Cromwell, astute and intelligent, was Henry's chief minister, while Cranmer held the post of Archbishop of Canterbury. In 1536, the Act of Suppression gave Henry the power to make his move on the smaller monasteries that had a declared income of less than £200 per year. Many of the buildings were sold to courtiers and the wealthy, while their valuable artefacts and possessions were made over to the crown.

With the second Act of Suppression in 1539 came the wholesale closure of monasteries, friaries, convents and priories, and with it the resultant loss of lands, wealth and employment. Even the sick had to go elsewhere as one by one the majority of the infirmaries and hospitals closed. The sale of the confiscated lands and property brought a great deal of money into the King's purse which was already filling up from the emptying of the religious houses of their valuables.

Opposition to the closures and the 'sacking' of the churches led to a great deal of civil unrest and the threat of rebellion was soon to become a reality. In Lincolnshire, an uprising began at Louth making its way to Lincoln where 40,000 people demanded change, while in the north of England a number of revolts took place that collectively became known as The Pilgrimage of Grace. For King Henry, this was a time of unprecedented civil disorder and danger.

Hostility to the reforms came from individuals as well as organised groups as they expressed their displeasure and disbelief. Early in 1535, Prior Robert Lawrence of Beauvale Priory (near to Moorgreen) and Prior Augustine Webster from Lincolnshire, journeyed to London to meet Prior John Houghton, previously of Beauvale, to discuss the events that had befallen them and to debate the Oath of Supremacy they were required to sign. Their request to Thomas Cromwell that they be exempt was refused and all three of them were incarcerated in the Tower of London and then put on trial for treason. Found guilty, the

Henry VIII.

The Pilgrimage of Grace.

three men were sentence to be hanged, drawn and quartered, and, along with two other unfortunates on 4 May, were taken to meet the executioner.

After being dragged through the streets on the hurdles to Tyburn, all five felons suffered the most horrific deaths. As his internal organs were being torn out, John Houghton is said to have cried out, 'Oh most Holy Jesus, have mercy on me in this hour' and, as the executioner pulled at his heart, Houghton again spoke, 'Good Jesus, what will you do with my heart?'

In that same year, three friars from Newark were arrested and cast into prison for their refusal to take the oath, two of them, Brother Hayfield and Hugh Payne are said to have died from the appalling treatment that they received while locked away in Marshalsea Gaol.

The Vicar of Newark, Henry Lytherland, was well aware of all that was going on around him and he quite probably knew the three men that had been placed in Marshalsea gaol, but this did not stop him from resisting the changes that were being imposed by the king's subordinates. For two more years, Lytherland stood firm in his beliefs until finally, in 1538, he was arrested on the charge of treason. Confined in a small, filthy, stinking cell within the castle prison at York he must have known his future prospects were for a show trial followed by a painful death at the hands of the executioner. The guilty verdict would have come as no surprise to Lytherand, and, on 2 August 1538, he was taken to the Knavesmire, outside York city walls, and hanged, drawn and quartered.

Lenton Priory also came under scrutiny in this same year when Prior Nicholas Heath and one of his monks were found guilty of treason and executed, either in Nottingham or in front of the Priory itself. One other monk and four labourers were executed later. The Prior of Thurgarton, on the other hand, was claimed to have committed adultery several times, and, after his monastery was surrendered to the Crown, he was given an annual pension of £40 a year, the tithes of two meadows of hay, a 'house called Fiskerton Hall', along with a garden and a stable. In all probability, the prior was a man of true faith and this accusation was only agreed to in order for him to escape death and to receive a suitable settlement.

In the end, Henry VIII broke from Rome, but, throughout the country as a whole, resistance to the changes had taken a heavy toll and perhaps none more so than in Nottinghamshire – as individuals stood up for their beliefs and ultimately paid for it with their lives.

After his diligent work in pushing through Henry's reforms, one man, from Nottinghamshire nonetheless, came out of this unfortunate time with more power and influence than he could possibly have dreamed of while growing up in a small rural village far away from the bustling streets of London – Thomas Cranmer, Archbishop of Canterbury.

Bloody Mary

Henry VIII's enduring legacy has been a country changed forever because of personal desires and wants, a place that was split down the middle into two distinct camps based on religion - Catholic and Protestant. He also left behind a country that lived in fear of choosing the wrong friends or allies, especially when it came to voicing an opinion about religion.

On his death the crown passed to his only son, Edward VI. This young boy shouldered the mantle of king at the tender age of nine and all looked well for a long and settled reign as he followed in his father's footsteps and championed the Protestant cause. It was Edward that took the decisions to finally sever most of the remaining links with the Catholic Church, as he passionately pressed ahead with yet more changes, and the architect behind these reforms was the Nottinghamshire 'boy done good', Thomas Cranmer of Aslockton.

In February 1553, Edward took ill and it was soon plain to see his illness was terminal. At the start of July, after just six years in power, Edward was dead and with him went the hopes of the Protestant cause. Before he died, he had tried to ensure the work of both him and his father would continue by trying to guarantee a Protestant succession of the throne when he named Lady Jane Grey (his cousin) as his rightful heir. His half sister, the Catholic Mary, had other ideas though. Gathering her forces of around 20,000 men at Framlingham Castle, Mary also claimed the crown for herself. After just nine days as Queen of England, the Protestant Jane was deposed by the Catholic Mary and, within months, young Jane had been sent to the scaffold where, at the tender age of sixteen, she lost her head.

Initially, Mary claimed that she would not compel her subjects to follow her chosen religion, yet, within weeks, Thomas Cranmer and others were arrested and imprisoned. It must have been obvious to Cranmer, and all those like him, that events would soon take a radical and terrible course. His refusal to tone down his beliefs in favour of those of the new queen and his belated and, perhaps reluctant, support for the deposed Queen Jane had led to his imprisonment in the Tower, and, on 13 November 1553, he and four others were put on trial for treason. The guilty verdict came as no surprise to those accused and Cranmer was sent back to prison to await developments.

March 1554 saw Thomas Cranmer moved to prison in Oxford, with him went two more one time Bishops, Nicholas Ridley and Hugh Latimer, each one knowing they would eventually pay the ultimate price. The arduous conditions and privations that all three men endured over the following months told as their health declined. The treatment they

Thomas Cranmer as a young man.   *The execution of Thomas Cranmer*

received both, physical and mentally, was designed to break their spirits and bring about recantations.

Ridley and Latimer were declared heretics and, on 16 October 1555, they were led out of their place of imprisonment and burnt at the stake. Cranmer was forced to watch the whole of this horrific spectacle from a nearby tower. The sight of his friends undergoing such a painful and abhorrent death had a profound effect on this elderly man who was, by now, sixty-six years old and in poor health.

In December, Cranmer was taken from his prison and put into more comfortable accommodation where over the next few weeks he made a number of recantations – renouncing a number of his beliefs. It was felt that his recantations did not go far enough so once again he was placed back in prison. His return into incarceration led to two more recantations, this time so far reaching that he once again claimed to embrace the Catholic religion – with his spirit finally broken he had submitted to the will of his accusers. For Queen Mary, nonetheless, this was not enough and she ordered that there should be no more postponements to his death sentence being carried out. Cranmer was told he would be allowed to speak just once more publicly during a service where he would make one last recantation as proof of his wrongdoings. Knowing the full horror of his fate he decided on a course of action that would show his supporters his true beliefs, when towards the end of his speech in the University Church he left the prepared script and renounced all the recantations he had made since his imprisonment, going as far as to say that the hand he had used to sign the papers would be the first to be punished at his impending execution. He next launched into an attack on the Pope claiming, amongst other things, that he was '[...] as Christ's enemy and Antichrist, with all his false doctrine', whereupon he was leaped upon and dragged from the pulpit and taken to the same spot that Latimer and Ridley had been executed on six months earlier.

Tied to the stake with an iron chain, the blaze starting to build and climb higher and higher, Thomas Cranmer plunged his right hand into the flames shouting out in a loud voice, 'This hand hath offendeth'. It was said that, such was his courage, he kept the 'offending hand' in the flames until it was a charred stump; not once did he move or flinch, except to wipe the sweat from his brow with his left hand. Minutes later, Cranmer was dead.

The Sorry Stuarts

During the time of Elizabeth I, the Catholics were, at times, vigorously suppressed, yet the difficulty of marriage to ensure the succession was always at the forefront of politics, because she did not know who she should marry. In the end, Elizabeth remained unmarried and without children or siblings to shoulder the mantle of monarch – on her death it was feared a power vacuum would be left behind and internal war and strife could follow if the wrong successor was chosen. The two contenders for the throne were Arbella Stuart and her cousin James Stuart, King of Scotland – both heirs in their own right. Even today, opinion is split over whom had the greatest claim to the throne, however, when Elizabeth died in March 1603, it was James that was invited to become King James I of England and not Arbella to be queen.

Highly educated and clearly intelligent, James seemed to have a knack of often forgetting how to put these skills to good use and he managed to earn himself the epithet of 'the wisest fool in Christendom' yet, for all his faults, James was the man of the hour. As he made his way southwards to London, he cleverly ennobled dozens of families by bribing them with titles – after all, the English and the Scots had been doing their best to kill each other for several hundred years, and now he was going to be the one in charge he needed them on his side. The grateful English snapped up these honours with pleasure and as his cavalcade made its way southwards the towns and villages on his route turned out en masse to get a look at this new king. His arrival in Nottinghamshire caused quite a stir, and, after indulging in a picnic as soon as he entered the county, he made his way to Worksop Manor where he was greeted by the Seventh Earl of Shrewsbury. It was at Worksop that James's mother, Mary Queen of Scots, had stayed for a short time while suffering from ill health and it was the Earl's father, the Sixth Earl, who had been her gaoler for many years. James was also well aware of the situation but his host managed to put on such a lavish spectacle all seemed to be forgiven.

The King's progress then took him through Tuxford and it is said that as the procession passed through the village he turned to one of his fellow travellers and enquired where he was. When he was told he was in Tuxford-in-the-Clay he retorted with the rather harsh remark that 'It should be Tuxford-in-the-Turd'.

It was when he reached Newark that the true nature of the King's character came to the fore. Like his unlucky royal predecessor, James took lodgings in the castle while staying in the town and much to his pleasure he found his surroundings very comfortable and pleasant. The omens seemed good when he was treated to a fine speech in Latin by Alderman Twentymans. Knowing that the King was especially fond of Latin, Twentymans had done his best to impress his sovereign by putting on an especially good show. The show went a little too well, for when the King asked the name of the Alderman he launched into a fit of anger. Some years earlier, a Twentymans had caused outrage when he had pulled down Redkirk in Scotland, believing the man in front of him was of the same family was too much for the King, who was bent on revenge. A few quick words from the unfortunate

Southwell, the Saracens Head.

Alderman quickly smoothed the way and he soon became one of the King's favourites.

Not everyone was as lucky as Twentymans during James' stay in Newark. A cutpurse had been caught red handed at his work and when knowledge of this reached the King's ears he issued a warrant that the criminal should be hanged straight away without any hearing or trial. This may have been seen by some of those that witnessed it as a foretaste of things to come under the rule of the Stuarts, and in many respects they would have been right.

Charles I's rise to power was one of those unfortunate accidents of history, simply because he was never destined to be a successful monarch. His inability to rule with the consent of the people led him to suspend Parliament on a number of occasions, and the on-off relationship he had with the House of Commons would ultimately lead to Civil War. In 1642, Charles made the fateful decision to raise his standard in Nottingham as a show of strength to Parliament, but the poor response to his call to arms amongst his supposedly faithful nobles and citizens must have been a dreadful blow to his pride. The Nottinghamshire noble families that did give their support would go on to lose most or all of their wealth in the forthcoming conflict, but it was the common folk that was to bear the brunt of the suffering. One of the first towns to declare for the king was Newark, yet again this strategically placed town was to play a part in the fortunes of a another monarch, who would never realise the suffering they would endure because of his actions.

Throughout the whole of the Civil War, Newark remained loyal to Charles and was besieged three times. The second siege was relieved by Prince Rupert in one of his most daring and clever manoeuvres, in such a way that the town was once more free from Parliamentarian threat. In 1644, the third and final siege began, and, by the middle of March 1646, Newark had been completely surrounded and cut off from the outside world, while inside the town plague had taken hold and its inhabitants were suffering terribly from illness and shortages of essentials.

King Charles realised that the war was lost and, making his way in disguise from his headquarters in Oxford, he travelled towards Newark to meet the head of the Scottish army that were encamped outside the town defences. Arriving at Southwell he rested briefly at the King's Head, now the Saracens Arms, before being taken to Lieutenant-General David Leslie, the acting head of the Scots, army where he surrendered. After talking to the Scots Commissioners he was asked to accompany them to their headquarters at Kelham for 'security' reasons. Lord Belasyse and the garrison at Newark only gave up the fight on the orders of Charles himself to surrender, and it was with a heavy heart that they complied.

On 1 January 1649, King Charles I went on trial charged as a 'tyrant, traitor and murderer; and a public and implacable enemy to the Commonwealth of England'. He was beheaded on 30 January. It would appear that Nottinghamshire, and in particular Newark, really did have some kind of effect on the Kings and Queens of this country.

The interregnum that followed has been described by many historians as a brief attempt at being a Republic, which ultimately failed when it was decided in 1660 to ask Charles II to return and to take up the reigns of Royal leadership. One asset that Charles II did have was a long memory and he most definitely had not forgotten the fate of his father, nor those that had caused his death. Fifty-nine men had signed Charles I death warrant and the new monarch was going to make sure they paid a heavy price for their involvement. Four Nottinghamshire men had been among those that put their signatures on the warrant and soon it would be their time to plead for their lives.

Colonel John Hutchinson, born in Nottingham, was arrested and first sent to Newark and then to the Tower in London before finally ending up in Sandown Castle near Folkestone. His property was confiscated and taken away and after eleven months of '[...] harsh and strict imprisonment without crime or accusation [...]', he died aged forty-nine.

General Henry Ireton, born in 1611 at Attenborough, married Oliver Cromwell's daughter and became one of his most trusted and able officers. Given various responsibilities, he died in Limerick in 1650 while holding the office of Lord Deputy in Ireland. His body was brought back to London for burial but even death did not save him from further punishment. What was left of his remains was dragged from its place of interment, the head being put on a pole for all to see, while his torso was hanged at Tyburn. Justice had to be seen to be done.

Gilbert Millington had been MP for Nottingham, with properties in Brinsley and at Felley Priory, near Annesley, and had been described as an unsavoury character with a disparaging manner. At his trial he apologised profusely for his behaviour over the death of Charles I, claiming he was carried along with the turmoil of the occasion and the power surrounding him. He was found guilty and sentenced to death. This was later commuted to life imprisonment with all his possessions confiscated. Millington died six years later on the island of Jersey aged seventy-six.

The last of the Nottinghamshire men to have signed Charles I death warrant was Major-General Edward Whalley from Screveton, a one-time Sheriff of Nottingham. He had stuck to his Parliamentary principals throughout the fighting and his regiment had been chosen to guard the King during his imprisonment at Hampton Court. When the King escaped, no blame was attached to the Major-General, but his most notorious act was to unhesitatingly put his name to the death warrant, With the restoration of Charles II to the throne, Whalley, and his son-in-law William Goffe (also a regicide), fled to New England, where they managed to evade capture. He was last seen alive in 1674 – an elderly man in poor health.

One other man from the county who was to play a very significant part in the execution of the King was Colonel Francis Hacker, born at East Bridgford and later of Colston Bassett. Hacker had been responsible for leading the king to the scaffold where he was beheaded, but the Colonel's ultimate fate was by far the worst suffered by any of those from Nottinghamshire that had been the cause of Charles demise. On 19 October 1660, after being found guilty and sentenced to death, he was taken to Tyburn and hanged, drawn and quartered. Some sources say that his son begged the new king for the return of his father's body which was granted before the corpse was quartered. His family also suffered when Charles II confiscated their lands and property and gave it to his younger brother James, Duke of York. The Duke saw an opportunity and sold the property back to the Hacker family for a large sum of money.

The Sorry Stuarts, it would appear, were not so sorry after all.

SELECT BIBLIOGRAPHY

Books

Andrews, William, *Bygone Punishments,* William Andrew and Co., London, 1899

Beardsmore, J.H., *The History of Hucknall Torkard,* J. Linney, 1909

Bennett, Michael, *Lambert Simnel and the Battle of Stoke,* Alan Sutton Publishing, Gloucester, 1987

Board, Joan, *The Great North Road Through Nottinghamshire,* The John Merrill Foundation, Waltham Cross, 2007

Brown, Cornelius, *A History of Nottinghamshire,* E. Stock, 1896

Brown, Cornelius, *Notes about Notts: A Collection of Singular Sayings, Curious Customs, Eccentric Epitaphs and Interesting Items,* T Forman and Sons, Nottingham, 1874

Burford, E.J., & Shulman, Sandra, *Of Bridles and Punishment, The Punishment of Women,* Robert Hale, London, 1994

Copnall, H. Hampton (Ed.), *Nottinghamshire County Records. Notes and Extracts from the Nottinghamshire County Records Office 17th Century,* Henry B Saxton, Nottingham, 1915

Dickinson, William, *The History and Antiquities of the Town of Newark in the County of Nottingham,* Longman, Hurst, Rees, Orme and Brown: Nichols and sons; and Baldwin, Cradock and Joy, 1819

Gill, Harry, *A Short History of Nottingham Castle,* 1904

Heathcote, Bernard V., *Viewing the Lifeless Body,* Nottinghamshire County Council, Nottingham, 2005

Holland Walker, J., *An Itinerary of Nottingham,* (Transactions of the Thoroton Society 29-35), 1925-1935

Lambley, Terry, *Nottingham: A Place of Execution from 1201 to 1928,* 1981

Moss, C., *East Retford and the Dukeries, A Handbook for Visitors and Residents,* 1908

Newbury, Elizabeth & Wood, Tim, *Punishment and Prisons,* Galleries of Justice. Nottingham, 1996

Page, William (Ed.), *A History of the County of Nottingham,* Constable, 1910

Stevenson, William, *Bygone Nottinghamshire,* Frank Murray, Nottingham 1893

Withers, Bill, *Nottinghamshire Constabulary: 150 Years in Photographs,* Quoin Publishing, Huddersfield, 1989

Archive Papers, Newspapers and Periodicals

British Parliamentary Papers. Crime and Punishment. Prisons.Vols 3,6,8,11. (Irish University Press 1970.

City of Nottingham (Police) Disciplinary Report Book

Creswell's Nottingham and Newark Journal

Criminal Register Indexes Vol. 13 (Dby/Ntt/Lin)

House of Commons Papers,Vol 31

Nottinghamshire Guardian 1850-1900

Southwell Workhouse Punishment Book (MSD/JS/101/1/3/11-472)

Transcriptions of the Deaconary Court of Nottingham 1565-1675 (Vols 1-2)

Other Sources

The Strangers Through the Town of Nottingham Being a Description of the Principal Buildings, and the Objects of Curiosity in that Town (Sutton and Son, Nottingham) 1827

Transactions of the Thoroton Society 21, (1917)

Transactions of the Thoroton Society 30, (1926)

Transactions of the Thoroton Society 32, (1928)

www.Binghamheritage.uk

www.Nottinghamshire.police.org.uk

www.Oldbaileyonline.org.uk

www.Southwellchurches.nottingham.ac.uk

If you enjoyed this book, you may also be interested in...

Haunted Mansfield

IAN MORGAN

This collection of stories contains both well-known and hitherto unpublished tales from around Mansfield. From the gruesome death of Bessie Shepherd, who sometimes walks the road on which she was murdered, to the White Lady of Newstead Abbey, Lord Byron's ancestral home, this spine-tingling selection of ghostly tales includes many pulse-raising narratives that are guaranteed to make your blood run cold. *Haunted Mansfield* will appeal to everyone with an interest in the supernatural history of this part of Nottinghamshire.

978 0 7524 5530 3

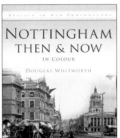

Nottingham Then & Now

DOUGLAS WHITWORTH

The city of Nottingham has seen significant changes to its buildings and streets over the centuries. From the first ever Boots chemist shop to the tram systems of two different centuries and the civic award-winning Short Stairs, the past continues to influence the present, and local historian Douglas Whitworth's selection of ninety-five new images, archive and modern, show just what has changed, and what has stayed the same. *Nottingham Then & Now* will appeal to all those who are interested in the city, past and present.

978 0 7524 6318 6

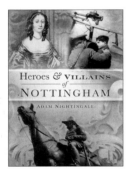

Heroes & Villains of Nottingham

ADAM NIGHTINGALE

This fascinating collection of biographies chronicles the lives of some of Nottingham's most famous (and in some cases infamous) personalities. Inside these pages, you will find Civil War legends such as Colonel John Hutchinson, Naval adventurer Edward Fenton – who sailed with the pirate Martin Frobisher in search of the Northwest passage – and Victoria Cross winning air aces. Illustrated with over eighty pictures, *Heroes & Villains of Nottingham* is a must-read for all those interested in the history of Nottingham.

978 0 7524 4924 1

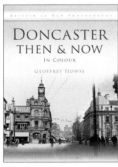

Doncaster Then & Now

GEOFFREY HOWSE

Doncaster thrived during the Georgian period, and continued to grow as a railway town in the nineteenth century. As a consequence, it can boast a rich architectural history, the influence of which can still be seen and appreciated in the fabric of the Doncaster of the modern day. Geoffrey Howse's comparisons between archive images of the Doncaster of decades past and modern photographs of the same scenes today beautifully illustrates the changing face of this historic city.

978 0 7524 6347 6

Visit our website and discover thousands of other History Press books.

www.thehistorypress.co.uk

The History Press